THE

PLOT
WHISPERER
BOOK OF
Writing Prompts

Easy Exercises to Get You Writing

MARTHA ALDERSON
Founder of PlotWriMo

Aadamsmedia

AVON, MASSACHUSETTS

DEDICATION

TO BOBBY RAY ALDERSON

Published by
Adams Media, a division of F+W Media, Inc.
57 Littlefield Street, Avon, MA 02322. U.S.A.
www.adamsmedia.com

ISBN 10: 1-4405-6081-1
ISBN 13: 978-1-4405-6081-1
eISBN 10: 1-4405-6082-X
eISBN 13: 978-1-4405-6082-8

Printed in the United States of America.

10   9   8   7   6   5   4   3   2   1

This book is available at quantity discounts for bulk purchases.
For information, please call 1-800-289-0963.

CONTENTS

ACKNOWLEDGMENTS

I am indebted to my remarkable editor, Peter Archer, and his vision for the Plot Whisperer series. The moment he suggested this prompt book, I knew it was the perfect complement to the other two plot books in the trilogy. Thank you to everyone at Adams Media for making this book come to life in such a short period of time. Special thanks to my agent Jill Corcoran for "discovering me."

I'd like to thank the women in my Wise Women group. Your belief in me drowns out the naysayers in my head. A special thanks to Cathy Cress. Time for the money chakra dance!

The prompts in this book are inspired by all the novels, memoirs, and screenplays I've analyzed and all the writers I've worked with over the years. I am deeply grateful to the authors of all those novels, memoirs, and screenplays and to all the writers who willingly have taken a leap of faith and tried the techniques and methods I put forward in this book. Your feedback and encouragement, successes and failures have been invaluable and have shaped the way I view plot and what it takes to write a story from beginning to end.

INTRODUCTION

You've got an idea. An idea for a novel, a short story, or perhaps a screenplay. You've thought about it for a long time, turning it over in your mind when you're driving to work, walking in the park, or sitting, late at night, watching the steam rise from a cup of tea.

And now you've taken the leap and decided to write. The force of the Universal Story that flows through you compels you to put pen to paper (or fingers to keyboard) and write.

But . . .

But you're stuck. You can't seem to get going. And what seemed so easy and so urgent now appears as a huge obstacle sitting in front of you, blocking your path to fulfillment.

So you've picked up this book.

The Plot Whisperer Book of Writing Prompts is written to help you with this problem—one, I can assure you, that is common to most writers. Be comforted; you're not alone. But you *do* need some help.

This book provides daily plot prompts guaranteed to move you from where you are in imagining and writing a novel, memoir, or screenplay to writing the story all the way to the end. The book is divided into four parts, corresponding to the various parts of your story:

The Beginning

This is where you and your protagonist first come to terms with the world you're creating. Here you:

- Identify the story's time and place
- Set up the dramatic action and underlying content that will run throughout the story
- Introduce the major characters
- Allude to the theme
- Introduce the protagonist's short-term goal and give a hint of her long-term goal

The Halfway Point

You're some distance along now, though still early in the story. You've established clearly for the reader the protagonist's long-term goal, as well as the antagonist(s) standing in her way. You've also discovered a cast of supporting characters who reflect back to the protagonist the elements she sees in others but cannot see in herself.

The Crisis

This, in many ways, is the emotional center of your story or novel. The protagonist undergoes her biggest challenge—a surge of energy that brings about both loss and transformation. Sometimes what she faces is death, though it may be something that seems less intense but is emotionally overwhelming.

The Climax and Resolution

Now the protagonist is ready to re-enter the world . . . but as someone who has been changed profoundly by her experience. The story's denouement is, for her, an end and a new beginning.

These four parts of the story are discussed at length in my book *The Plot Whisperer: Secrets of Story Structure Any Writer Can Master.*

The Three Prompts

Turn to the section that best represents where you are in your story. For example, if you are beginning a new story, you'll start at "The Beginning." Each of the four parts of the book is divided into thirty prompt sets.

Each set contains three prompts:

1. A daily affirmation designed to help raise your energy to write.
2. A plot element to prompt your imagination and expression toward the plot and structure considerations at the exact spot where you are in writing your story.
3. A writing prompt that gives a specific exercise, the object of which is to get you to write something that advances the plot of your story.

Cycle through the prompts and write every day until you finish your story. I can't stress enough the importance of developing a regular writing habit. For some writers, finishing takes ten years. For other writers, the cycle lasts merely a few months. Follow as many or as few prompts as serves you each day. For writers who wish to use this book to support their month-long writing frenzy during NaNoWriMo—the national challenge to write a 50,000-word novel in thirty days—follow at least four prompts daily to reach the final prompt on the last day of the month.

The book is structured to take you from your own unique beginning to the end as the book cycles through the four stages of the Universal Story that has no beginning and is without end.

Create a Ritual

Reading these three prompts daily becomes a ritual to prime yourself for writing. This ritual provides a means to express your creativity more fully. Ceremonial rites stimulate creativity and reward you with greater self-expression, self-discovery, and self-exploration.

As one day grows out of the day before and becomes tomorrow, every time you open this book, read a prompt, and then write, you work in partnership with your creativity and imagination and increase your overall confidence level. Every word you write every day strengthens the power of the ritual; this in turn clears the way forward to write a story from beginning to end.

THE DAILY AFFIRMATION

To write takes confidence and energy. Each day you open this book, you find an affirmation reminding you of your goals. Each time you renew your commitment to yourself, you renew your energy for your story. The more committed and highly energized you are, the more successful you'll be. Suddenly, the ritual of showing up for your dreams empowers you to seize that which you most want.

Something haunts you—a line of dialogue, a character; an event whispers to you like an invitation to sit down and write. Imagine for a moment that perhaps something in the invisible world wishes to manifest in the visible world. You—yes, *you*—have been chosen to make that dream a reality. You can always say no. However, once you say yes, the confidence and commitment you bring to that task is sure to rise and fall as you follow the path on which your story leads you.

Some writers find emotional support in a writing group. Other writers swing privately from one dark mood to another, even darker one. You, on the other hand, will find support in the affirmations in this book.

Learning new concepts and exploring new ideas can fill or deplete you of energy. Daily affirmations lift your vigor, refocus your beliefs in yourself, and keep you writing. The ritual of repeating an affirmation every day at the same time becomes the anchor that keeps you grounded when life and your story fall apart around you.

The affirmations provide inspiration and foster creativity as you follow the other two daily prompts into the more concrete plot elements of writing your story from beginning to end. Every day you open this book and repeat an affirmation, you are symbolically focusing your thoughts on your goals. You become immersed in the specific steps of writing what needs to be written today. Daily repetition of an affirmation builds positive, upbeat energy.

THE PLOT ELEMENT PROMPT

The aim of this book is to support you in finishing what you start. Writing while keeping plot and structure in mind helps you accomplish that and completes the cycle from inspiration to manifestation. At least your part of that cycle is done.

You are committed to write. So write a story. Write a beginning, a middle, and an end. Write a story in which the protagonist transforms and the action is always exciting. Weave subplots into the primary plot. Write a story with meaning.

The second prompt in each prompt set is based on the energetic expectations for the particular point at which you find yourself in the Universal Story. The suggestions are broad enough to allow your own individual expression to emerge in a pleasing form for the reader. Those of you who have read *The Plot Whisperer* know that every story contains four scenes or moments that serve as turning points in which energy surges enough to turn the dramatic action of the story in a new direction. I call these energetic markers. As you move forward with your story, you'll need to identify these markers. The plotting prompts given here are a way of helping you do that.

While following the plot prompts in this book, no stream of consciousness writing is allowed, *unless it applies directly to the advancement of the plot of your story.* Don't write fragments, unless the fragments hold the promise of entire scenes. Everything, in other words, must be at the service of the plot.

A writer's life, like the character's journey, is cyclical. Daily plot prompts stimulate a specific plot element for the specific point in the cycle where you are right now—in the middle of a story, dreaming of a new story while sending out queries for the first one, or ready for a rewrite.

Focusing on one specific plot element every day keeps you on track to achieve your goal of writing a novel. The plot prompts in this book provide a container for your words.

I said that this book will help you finish what you start. But don't hold a narrow definition of "finish." Writing one draft from beginning to end is finishing. Rewriting your story from beginning to end is finishing. Seeing your work published is finishing. You decide what constitutes a complete writing cycle for you. The plot prompts in this book guide you to your story's end.

THE WRITING PROMPT

Finishing happens when you write consistently. Consistency creates habits and routines. Some habits are unconscious; some you are aware of. Some routines are self-destructive; others promote good health. Every time you write repeatedly with strong purpose, intention, and emphasis, the habit or routine enters the realm of a ritual.

In my time as a plot consultant and teacher, I've met writers who talk about writing but don't actually write. I've met others who write endlessly but never get anywhere. In both cases, it usually means that the person doesn't know what to write next. She struggles for something that will enhance the overall plot and structure of her story. The writing prompts in this book take care of that for you.

The most important element in this entire book is *daily writing*. You decide how long you write every day and how many words you write based on developing your own personal writing goal (see the last section of this Introduction for the steps). At first your writing feels awkward and self-conscious. That's okay. Establish a routine of writing at a specific time of the day, every day. Imprinting a writing habit comes before judging what you have written. Become organized and structured before turning your full attention to the words you write. (This idea echoes in your writing: first ensure that the plot and structure are in place before turning your full attention to writing the specific details.)

The writing prompts center on writing scenes and summaries. Each one defines your short-term writing goal for the day. Short-term goals are good for you, like an unconditional promise weaving through your writing day in and day out until you reach your long-term goal of finishing your novel, memoir, or screenplay from beginning to end.

The plot prompt stimulates your logical mind. The writing prompt structures your imaginary mind. After reading the writing prompt, you may find yourself gazing out the window . . . or you may begin writing. Each day, begin a new scene or continue writing the scene you started during the previous writing session. You decide based on what serves your story the best.

Write one scene at a time. If you've read *The Plot Whisperer*, use the scenes you created, plotted, and tracked during your perusal; or simply start anywhere and write as you go. Layer plot prompts over several days.

Every day that you repeat the ritual of writing at the same time, you awaken a greater realization of connectedness to all of the energies of the universe supporting you in achieving your writing goals.

How to Use This Book

Writing merely for the sake of putting words to paper may produce a piece that is simply sublime. However, if your goal is to write a full-blown novel, memoir, or screenplay that readers and audiences will enjoy, write toward the completion and do not stop until you reach your goal. Writing one story with the intention of finishing allows those sublime moments to rise to the surface. And, in the end, you hold a finished novel.

In character-driven stories and virtually all women's fiction, the protagonist is emotionally affected by her past and the people who raised her. Thus, women's fiction often centers on relationships and includes multiple-viewpoint characters, each of whom change or transform on some level. The writing prompts in this book center on a protagonist. Traditionally, she is the character most changed by the dramatic action of a story. Thus, a story that involves several protagonists shows each of them transform at the end. If you prefer to use more than one protagonist, complete the prompts in this book with the full cast of protagonists in mind at all times.

Decide which character will assume the role of the protagonist in which scenes. Switch back and forth between the characters and assign them the exercises that feel most appropriate to that character and your story. Alternately, complete the prompts more than once, each time with a different character.

The more prompts you follow and the deeper into your story you write, the more you will appreciate that one character does indeed transform more than all the rest—the one true protagonist.

This is a book for writers who are ready to commit to their writing. That's a big step. Really committing to your writing is a bit like a marriage: you don't know at the beginning exactly how it's going to work out, but you're willing to take a chance, opening up a part of yourself that until now has been secret. Possibly at this point you don't even know exactly what you want to write about . . . you just know you want to—*need to*—write. You'll benefit from practical support and guidance, and accountability. This book keeps you on track as you write your novel, memoir, or screenplay.

Let's assume that you understand why you want to write. Perhaps you've read *The Plot Whisperer* and are aware of some of the many pitfalls when writing a complete story. From filling out forms, answering questions, plotting your story, and tracking your scenes in *The Plot Whisperer Workbook*, you know how to write a novel, memoir, or screenplay.

Now comes the time to make the leap. It's time to write.

WHERE AND WHEN

Determine the most optimum time to perform the ritual of reading and following the prompts in this book. Prepare a place to perform the rites and to write. It should be somewhere in which you feel comfortable and centered and can marshal your thoughts and your energy. Pick a place where you're not likely to be interrupted or distracted. Remember, writing is what *you* want to do, so you need a space that can become *you*.

WHAT

The prompts are short and do not employ any intricate tools. All that is required of your ritual is a means to write your story—pad of paper and pencil, computer . . . you decide. A mirror is helpful but not necessary (affirmations are especially powerful when uttered aloud to yourself in front of a mirror). No prompts employ any elaborate costumes. Wear what is most comfortable and what makes you feel most like yourself.

MUSIC

Music can enhance your relaxation and encourage deep writing. Rhythm is the pulse of life and can help calm emotions and aid in the exploration of imagination and creativity. There aren't any prescriptions for what kind of music you should listen to; just pick something that relaxes you and makes you feel creative.

NATURE

Some sort of nature or the outdoors in or around your ritual and writing space is beneficial. You don't have to write outside, but it's nice if you can look out a window while you're at work.

A Link to Yourself

This book is meant to support you, motivate you, and inspire you to keep writing. As I wrote in *The Plot Whisperer*, writing takes you on a journey that is often similar to the one undertaken by your protagonist.

You write to evoke strong emotions in the reader. You deliberately knock the energy of the story out of balance in order to force the protagonist to struggle against antagonists. The more out of balance the energy, the more excitement on the page and the better able the reader is to gain a full picture of who the character is. The interplay between antagonist and protagonist creates a new state, a new life, a new completeness, and a new story.

When exploring strong emotions in your characters, you often find that you've aroused similar emotions in yourself. Quickly, your energy falters. This means that something inside you is out of balance.

In optimum circumstances, your inner energy is composed of two equal yet opposite forces, Yin and Yang. The Yang force is responsible for expanding and reaching outward. The Yin is responsible for the contraction or pulling inward. To stay in perfect balance between the two forces is so difficult that an imbalance is nearly inevitable. Expansion adds volume without equal contraction. Conversely, too much contraction means not enough reaching out. When your energy is out of balance, you have either too much or too little. The two forces struggle with each other in the drive to return to your original state of balance and harmony.

Allow strong emotions to dominate you and you slow your progress toward the successful completion of your goal. However, you can't shut such emotions out; you will experience them. When you do so and when you see or sense emotion coming from someone else, pay attention. Listen carefully. Observe your own actions and the actions of others. Take a guess at the true root cause of the pain and then ask yourself what drew you to that conclusion. Use what you learn from this to convey emotion in your characters (however, do so without resorting to telling the reader what the characters are feeling; instead *show* it through their actions and dialogue).

The affirmations in this book connect you to and strengthen your true and balanced self.

Read the Prompts

I spoke earlier about the power of ritual. Rituals can help you integrate the positive with learning and taking action. This in turn leads to emotional balance. The more emotionally balanced you are, the more confident and open you will be to creativity. This is yet another reason to establish a regular habit of reading the three prompts together every day. Welcome encouragement, support, and guidance at every step of your journey to make your dream of writing a book a reality.

Creating a Personal Writing Goal

Along this journey, you need to establish milestones to mark your progress. One of the most important of these is a personal writing goal. The following steps help you determine how many words to write daily, with a fixed deadline in mind.

1. Decide when you would like to complete this full draft of your story. (After you determine the number of words you'll need to write daily, you may find that you want to reconsider your deadline. If so, recalculate Step 3.)
2. Visit an independent bookstore, a chain, or Amazon.com. Find three books vaguely similar to yours. Jot down the page count.
3. Multiply the average number of pages in the three books you chose by 250 words per page. Based on your deadline and the number of words you need to write from the beginning of your story to the end, calculate how many words per day are needed to reach your goal.

Projected ending date: _____

Total number of words for your story: _____

Daily word count writing goal is: _____

If you're not concerned with a specific deadline, consider instead basing your short-term goals on the number of pages you write daily or try writing for a specified amount of time, using an egg timer.

PART I

THE BEGINNING

The concepts used in the daily plot and writing prompts in "The Beginning" support you in crafting the beginning of your novel, memoir, or screenplay. For more in-depth information about the plot and structure points used in this section, view the videos devoted to crafting the beginning of a story on Martha Alderson's free YouTube channel *www .youtube.com/user/marthaalderson*.

Read the sections about the plot elements necessary for every great beginning in *The Plot Whisperer* (Chapters 2, 3, and 4), *The Plot Whisperer Workbook* (Chapters 1 through 5), and *Blockbuster Plots: Pure & Simple*.

While reading and following the prompts for this first quarter of the book, mull over ideas about who the protagonist is now compared to who you imagine she may become at the end of the book. The scenes in the first quarter of the story culminate at the first Energetic Market: The End of the Beginning Scene.

Figure 1. The Plot Planner: Above and Below

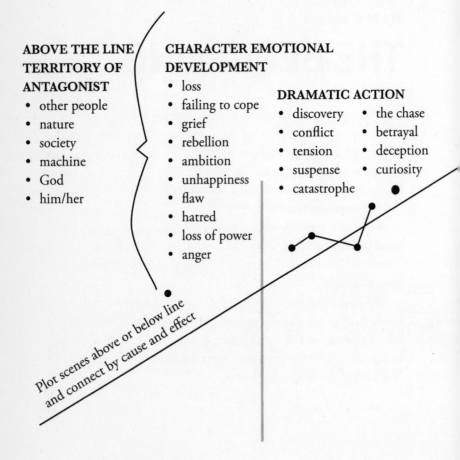

ABOVE THE LINE TERRITORY OF ANTAGONIST
- other people
- nature
- society
- machine
- God
- him/her

CHARACTER EMOTIONAL DEVELOPMENT
- loss
- failing to cope
- grief
- rebellion
- ambition
- unhappiness
- flaw
- hatred
- loss of power
- anger

DRAMATIC ACTION
- discovery
- conflict
- tension
- suspense
- catastrophe
- the chase
- betrayal
- deception
- curiosity

Plot scenes above or below line and connect by cause and effect

BEGINNING (1/4)

THEMATIC SIGNIFICANCE
- mood
- metaphor
- sensory details
- setting
- define
- development
- mention

DRAMATIC ACTION
- lull in conflict
- giving info
- telling

CHARACTER EMOTIONAL DEVELOPMENT
- calm
- coping
- planning
- solving problems
- contemplative
- in control

BELOW THE LINE: TERRITORY OF PROTAGONIST

MIDDLE (1/2)

END (1/4)

PROMPT 1

AFFIRMATION PROMPT

I willingly expand and reach outward with my writing and, at the same time, contract and pull inward for answers and calm. The balance within me is perfect. (Close your eyes and take a couple of deep breaths.)

Today I write.

PLOT PROMPT

Your protagonist wants something. Her desires and needs create her long-term goal (something she either thinks she can have or that she cannot have). Your protagonist's short- and long-term goals create scenes showing the steps she takes forward toward the completion of her goal or how she is pushed backward away from success.

Often, the protagonist's long-term goal is implied at the beginning of stories rather than fixed. Dramatic action causes the protagonist to react, which, in turn, forms her first stated or overt goal. Characters need definable action through which to express their emotions.

Mark on a Plot Planner for your story a scene in which the protagonist establishes a short- and/or long-term goal.

WRITING PROMPT

Write a scene that shows your main character taking action toward her goal. For instance, she looks through the want ads for a job. She shows her own style and voice in how she searches for a job or a partner, attempts to solve a mystery, tries to write a book, attempts to get from one place to another, or something else. Whatever you write should clearly illustrate your protagonist's voice and her attitude. If she is the narrator, the writing should reveal her inner voice as well as her external one.

RECORD

Record the time you start writing: _____

Record the time you stop writing: _____

Total number of words you wrote today: _____

Daily writing goal is: _____

Projected ending date: _____

Like taking your temperature, take a minute to assess your energy level now that you have finished writing. High energy (excited, joyful, positive, energized, inspired) is a 10. Low energy (depressed, anxious, sad, negative, sluggish) is a 1.

Energy level: _____

Review the Character Emotional Development Profile for your protagonist. Assess how many traits and attributes of the protagonist you showed in today's scene.

PROMPT 2

AFFIRMATION PROMPT

Today I take action. I sit where I most like to write. While I write, I hydrate my imagination by drinking water (or some other thirst-quenching drink). I tune out everything but the sound of words appearing on the page from out of nowhere.

Today I write.

PLOT PROMPT

A sense of place grounds a reader in the here and now of a story. The place or setting of a story becomes one half of the relationship between the protagonist and the world around her. Relationships of all kinds—in this case, with the setting—provide insight into the character beyond what the character may believe about herself through the interactions she has with others. Plot a scene showing how the story's environment affects the protagonist's feelings, actions, and behavior in order to help define her.

Chart your scene above the Plot Planner line or your own chart if the protagonist is not in control of what is happening in her surroundings, or below the line if there is little to no conflict, tension, or suspense and the protagonist is in control.

WRITING PROMPT

Incorporate into the action you wrote in the first prompt a sense of where the action takes place. For now, forget the details. Write a passage that gives a bird's-eye view of the place—a city, the country, outer space, the desert, a bright shopping district, a slum, a dark alley, in the middle of the ocean. Create an overview sense of the place for grounding, one that shows a broad connection between the protagonist and the setting.

If you are writing a mystery, this bird's-eye view can be an overview of the mystery itself more than the actual physical location of the story.

RECORD

Record the time you start writing: _____

Record the time you stop writing: _____

Total number of words you wrote today: _____

Daily writing goal is: _____

Projected ending date: _____

Energy level: _____

PROMPT 3

AFFIRMATION PROMPT

Blind faith leads me to believe that words flow effortlessly every day. My part is simply to sit down and write.

Today I write.

PLOT PROMPT

A character pursuing her goal does not by herself create action that is dramatic. What creates drama is her encounter with obstacles that interfere with her movement toward that goal. That's especially true when the character stands to lose something significant if she's unable to reach her goal.

The most exciting and dramatic relationships in stories are those that involve an antagonist. Antagonists interfere with the protagonist's quest for her goal. They create obstacles, confusion, and diversions. Scenes between the protagonist and her antagonist(s) create tension, conflict, and curiosity. Readers turn the pages faster when reading scenes that involve a formidable antagonist or the possibility of one showing up. Plot such a scene on your Plot Planner.

WRITING PROMPT

Your protagonist takes the next step toward her short-term goal. Write moment-by-moment action as someone or something stands in her way and interferes with her getting what she wants.

Take time to introduce this new character. Show the character in such a way that the reader will remember and differentiate between this character, the protagonist, and all the other characters to come. Assign the character a foible, a quirk, special clothing, abilities, a physical trait, and/or a distinctive speaking style.

Use dialogue.

If the protagonist has a special ability, show a hint of what it is now.

RECORD

Record the time you start writing: _____

Record the time you stop writing: _____

Total number of words you wrote today: _____

Daily writing goal is: _____

Projected ending date: _____

Energy level: _____

Review the Character Emotional Development Profile (for more discussion of this, see *The Plot Whisperer*, Chapter 3) for the antagonist. Assess how many traits and attributes you showed of the antagonist in today's scene.

PROMPT 4

AFFIRMATION PROMPT

I respect my writing commitment by scheduling around my daily chores and responsibilities and alerting others about my uninterrupted writing time.

Today I write.

PLOT PROMPT

Start your story at a moment of significant change and you immediately invite the reader into the main action of the story. Conceive of a scene in which your protagonist, antagonist, supporting character(s), or the setting itself undergoes an important change.

In most scenes with an antagonist, the antagonist is in control. If that is the case with your scene, plot your scene above the Plot Planner line or your own chart. If the protagonist is in control of what is happening, plot the scene below the line.

WRITING PROMPT

Usually scenes where the protagonist is in control have little to no conflict, tension, or suspense unless threatened by an antagonist. The previous writing prompt directed you to show your protagonist confronted by someone or something standing in the way of her goal. Because of what happens in that scene, write the actions the protagonist takes now that her fear, flaw, hatred, or prejudice has been activated, set off, provoked, or sparked.

Show how the protagonist usually reacts to such a challenge and the actions she takes when she is stopped, blocked, or prevented from reaching her goal. Show her emotional reaction by her behavior, her body language, the words she speaks, and what she neglects or refuses to say.

RECORD

Record the time you start writing: _____

Record the time you stop writing: _____

Total number of words you wrote today: _____

Daily writing goal is: _____

Projected ending date: _____

Energy level: _____

PROMPT 5

AFFIRMATION PROMPT

I deserve the time it takes to write a novel. I take this time for me. The time I take away from others, from other actions, and from the outside world I use well.

Today I write.

PLOT PROMPT

Every story is made up of subplots that are thematically tied to the primary plot about whether the protagonist will achieve her goal . . . or not. One major subplot in stories is often a romance plot. Depending on what type of story you are writing, this romance plot can be themed around friendship, a partnership, or love. Determine the romantic subplot in your story.

WRITING PROMPT

Two characters meet who represent the romantic plot. Write a front story scene between the two that is uncluttered with backstory information about either one of them. Make every word choice emphasize only the information the reader needs to make sense of the protagonist as she interacts with the other character while striving toward her goal. Push to the background all nonessential information.

Keep the reader ever alert as to why the characters are taking action and how that action advances each toward his or her own competing goals.

No matter how at odds the two characters may be or whatever the lack of sexual tension between them when first introduced, show the romantic subplot's capacity for creating longing and love in the protagonist.

It is still early in the story and your reader is still determining who is important to the story and whose story this is. Provide clues to support the reader in his or her determination.

✍ RECORD

Record the time you start writing: _____

Record the time you stop writing: _____

Total number of words you wrote today: _____

Daily writing goal is: _____

Projected ending date: _____

Energy level: _____

PROMPT 6

AFFIRMATION PROMPT

I believe in an abundance of all things. Everything I commit to in life, I get. I commit to keep writing until I finish my story.

Today I write.

PLOT PROMPT

The thematic significance of a story shows what all the words in each scene add up to. At its best, the significance of a story connects each reader and audience member to a moment of clarity about our shared relationship to a bigger picture through a wider complex of thoughts and relationships that exist outside the story.

The thematic significance of a story is a statement illustrated and supported by the writing. Until you know your story and what your story conveys, stick to discovering the various themes. Every story communicates its own unique pattern of themes and ideas.

WRITING PROMPT

Themes emerge while you're writing your scenes. Support the concepts in scenes through the use of mood and tone, voice and word choices, metaphors and similes, and details.

Match the tone and pace of the scenes you write with the story themes. A bleak story about revenge moves at a different pace and with a different tone than does a hopeful story about redemption.

Show the protagonist doing something she is good at as it relates to the overall plot. See what happens. Write that.

RECORD

Record the time you start writing: _____

Record the time you stop writing: _____

Total number of words you wrote today: _____

Daily writing goal is: _____

Projected ending date: _____

Energy level: _____

Review the Character Emotional Development Profile for the love interest character. Assess how many traits and attributes you showed of that character in today's scene.

Plot your scene above or below the line on a Plot Planner or your own chart.

PROMPT 7

AFFIRMATION PROMPT

I draw the rhythm of my day from this ritual of raising my energy, practicing plot, and daily writing.

Today I write.

PLOT PROMPT

Sense organs relay messages to your brain: the smell of dust on the road, the taste of rust, the heat of the summer sun beating on your skin.

A setting bathed in sights and sounds, language and climate, draws the reader in at the sensory level. Sensory details, fully realized, reinforce the deeper meaning of a story and evoke emotion.

Before each character is a world only she sees and imagines. The trick to creating a memorable character is finding something special in or about her that makes her "her." What she attends to in the plethora of details surrounding her reflects *her* feelings, ones that show life differently than it is depicted in other stories. Only she feels about her life the way she does. Only she sees and hears the world around her in the way she does. Such individuality creates a sense of mystery around each character.

WRITING PROMPT

Earlier, you created a broad idea of the setting and the protagonist's relationship to it. Now, vary the situation your main character is in and write about what she is doing in the here and now of the story. As always, ground the character and the reader by providing sensory details of the story world.

Highlight those features that provide insight about the protagonist. From all the visual, auditory, and tactile stimulation around her, show what the protagonist notices about how her world tastes and smells that sets her apart and gives an inkling about who she was before becoming who she is now. Don't *tell* the reader how her backstory shapes her beliefs and expectations of life, as well as her life direction; *show* us out of everything else, the sensory details that most draw the protagonist's attention.

RECORD

Record the time you start writing: _____

Record the time you stop writing: _____

Total number of words you wrote today: _____

Daily writing goal is: _____

Projected ending date: _____

Energy level: _____

Plot your scene above or below the line on a Plot Planner or your own chart.

PROMPT 8

AFFIRMATION PROMPT

A force deep within me pulls me forward and keeps me clear and focused on the writing task at hand. I write to better my word count every day.

Today I write.

PLOT PROMPT

A core plot of your story revolves around your protagonist's inner development. To satisfy this inner plot, the protagonist must undergo a deep and fulfilling transformation. You accomplish this by exposing to the reader the character's inevitable flaws. In the latter part of the story, she will have to face her largest flaw and overcome it in order to achieve her ultimate goal.

Scan earlier scenes for examples of the protagonist's chief character flaw. If she acts in one scene like a victim, unable to take responsibility for her actions, develop that aspect of her. If she appears controlling in one scene or you find her argumentative in another, or she lies in one scene and cheats in another, use her stubbornness and need to always be right to your advantage. Pin her with that flaw.

Perfectionist, procrastinator, judgmental, quick-tempered, angry: Every one of these flaws allows for a different character emotional development and transformation, and yet every one is universal within the human race.

WRITING PROMPT

Demonstrate the character's flaw as she takes another step toward her goal. Show how she interferes and sabotages her own progress to the reader. However, keep this self-reflective insight a secret from the protagonist until after the crisis, about three quarters of the way through the story.

Show how the protagonist's flaw manifests itself in her typical actions in contrast to how you imagine she may behave later in the story.

Try using all dialogue first and fill in the action later.

RECORD

Record the time you start writing: _____

Record the time you stop writing: _____

Total number of words you wrote today: _____

Daily writing goal is: _____

Projected ending date: _____

Energy level: _____

Change the Character Emotional Development Profile for your protagonist so that it reflects what you're learning about your character.

Plot your scene above the line on a Plot Planner. When the protagonist is under the spell of her flaw, she is in conflict.

PROMPT 9

AFFIRMATION PROMPT

The ideas come and my writing flows easily. I detach from my ego and surrender my judgment of good and bad. Every day, I write.

Today I write.

PLOT PROMPT

A story is about a character transformed over time by the dramatic action. In order to make this character transformation more dramatic, convey who the character is within the safety of a world that is familiar to her before she is thrust into a new world.

The ordinary world gives the reader insight into the values, background, and habits of the protagonist (or lack thereof). An understanding of the protagonist's ordinary world gives the reader a starting point from which to evaluate the emotional change in the protagonist as she is forced to break away and rely on herself in the middle of the story.

In her usual life, customs, dogma, rules, and regulations come from outside her. They often form a kind of inner protection for her, shielding her from unpleasant truths she doesn't want to acknowledge. In the middle of the story, when this protection is stripped away, she becomes vulnerable. If we grasp the comfortable, safe, and well-fed environment the protagonist has always known, it's easier for us to sympathize when she wonders why she left it in pursuit of a solitary, difficult, and dangerous new world.

WRITING PROMPT

The protagonist moves toward her goal, acting as she is accustomed to doing. Show how those around her usually treat her and to what the protagonist is most attached. Her set of beliefs, material goods, behaviors, and the degree of her attachment will foreshadow the degree of difficulty she'll experience when she must detach and move out of the beginning into the middle of the story.

Give only the most important details about elements that are pivotal to the overall plot. Keep the story moving forward. Save the information you wish the reader to remember in detail for later in the story.

Deepen what you have written so far about the protagonist and what she does, while also remaining consistent to the character you first introduced.

Edit and develop ideas as you write.

RECORD

Record the time you start writing: _____

Record the time you stop writing: _____

Total number of words you wrote today: _____

Daily writing goal is: _____

Projected ending date: _____

Energy level: _____

Plot your scene above or below the line on a Plot Planner or your own chart.

PROMPT 10

AFFIRMATION PROMPT

I find unusual people in unexpected places help me keep to my daily writing goals.

Today I write.

PLOT PROMPT

Allies support the protagonist's forward movement. Of course, they have their own personal goals beyond the function they serve directly. Allies' goals often reflect the protagonist's goals but with their own particular twist. Allies' goals often reflect what the protagonist thinks she wants. The secondary characters' active pursuit of their goals creates a subplot, especially when these goals come into conflict with those of the protagonist.

WRITING PROMPT

As your protagonist moves, either stumbling or striding, toward her goal, continue to show that special attitude, trait, behavior, posture, and/or ability that makes her unique. Remind the reader what makes the protagonist "her." Now show a different side of her.

Introduce an outside force, another character, an ally, stepping in to help keep her on track toward her goal.

Say yes to the first idea that comes to you about the ally and then write how that person interacts with the protagonist. A resounding "yes!" starts the plot line going.

Plant something the protagonist dreams of having or doing that is beyond her ability to seize for herself, here in the beginning. She dreams about it, but would need the help of an outside force or a bit of magic in order to be successful.

✎ RECORD

Record the time you start writing: _____

Record the time you stop writing: _____

Total number of words you wrote today: _____

Daily writing goal is: _____

Projected ending date: _____

Energy level: _____

Plot your scene above or below the line on a Plot Planner or your own chart.

PROMPT 11

AFFIRMATION PROMPT

Reading this affirmation, studying plot, and writing bring me joy. Reading affirmations, studying plot, and writing daily bring out the best in me.

Today I write.

PLOT PROMPT

Whether a spiritual belief or a coping strategy, a physical ailment or society at large, every antagonist has one primary goal within the context of the story: to prevent or delay the protagonist from successfully reaching her goal. Antagonists always interfere with the protagonist's forward progress.

Beyond merely opposing the protagonist, antagonists have their own personal goals. Antagonists' goals are usually in direct opposition to the protagonist's goal.

The antagonist's active pursuit of her goal creates a subplot.

WRITING PROMPT

Describe the major antagonist(s) facing the protagonist. Reveal only enough of the background information about the protagonist and antagonist as is necessary for the reader to make sense of the scene (save most of the memories and, if you must, flashbacks for scenes in the middle).

Imagine an adventure that feels linked to the previous action or action to come. Write what you envision with curiosity and attention as the antagonist moves along. Allow yourself to be surprised by what you write.

Hint at the dark side of the antagonist but show elements of a lighter side in such a way as to leave the reader wondering who the antagonist really is inside.

RECORD

Record the time you start writing: _____

Record the time you stop writing: _____

Total number of words you wrote today: _____

Daily writing goal is: _____

Projected ending date: _____

Energy level: _____

Change the Character Emotional Development Profile you filled out for the antagonist to reflect what you're learning about that character as you write.

Plot your scene above the line on your Plot Planner or your own chart.

PROMPT 12

AFFIRMATION PROMPT

I daily write words in pursuit of my goal. Every day, I record my word count and joyfully acknowledge my progress forward.

Today I write.

PLOT PROMPT

A character flaw is a coping mechanism that arises from the loss of an original state of perfection that occurred in the character's backstory. Her flaw is designed to compensate for perceived vulnerability and a sense of insecurity. No matter how confident, every major character demonstrates lessons learned from the wound inflicted in her backstory that are now lodged in her core belief system.

For now, develop the character's front story information. The front story is the one that drives the action in the scene on the page. Leave all details of the protagonist's backstory and/or backstory wound for development in the middle.

The more contrast between the front story laid out in the beginning and the backstory deepened in the middle, the more exciting the story.

WRITING PROMPT

As the protagonist takes what she believes is another step nearer to her goal, show how her actions cause conflict or suffering for someone or something else.

Today, write a scene without revealing any background information —leave out all memories and flashbacks. Write only the action that the protagonist takes in the front story in pursuit of her goal. Omit or keep way in the background anything not essential to today's particular scene. Let the reader fill in the blanks about her past for now. Make the reader wonder how the protagonist came to have such unique or different traits or reactions, and turn the pages to find out the answer.

Convey how a trait within her—strength, fear, prejudice, love, weakness, or something else—causes the conflict or suffering in someone else. Trust your imagination and come up with a situation that feels thematically true to your story. Write about whatever floats into your mind.

RECORD

Record the time you start writing: _____

Record the time you stop writing: _____

Total number of words you wrote today: _____

Daily writing goal is: _____

Projected ending date: _____

Energy level: _____

Plot your scene above or below the line on a Plot Planner or your own chart.

PROMPT 13

AFFIRMATION PROMPT

I choose daily to keep writing.

Today I write.

PLOT PROMPT

In the beginning quarter of the story, get the front story going first by hooking readers and audiences with present, moment-to-moment conflict. The protagonist faces an immediate dilemma, experiences a loss, feels fear, and is compelled to take action.

The beginning introduces all aspects of the characters who play defining roles in your story, roles that you plan to deepen in the middle.

WRITING PROMPT

Heighten the conflict you wrote about earlier between the protagonist and someone or something else. Show how the protagonist reacts to the misunderstanding, setback, drama, fight, or loss caused by the conflict. Show us all sides of her.

Write only the action the protagonist takes in the front story in pursuit of her goal.

Don't wait for the exactly right action idea to come to you. Write the things you imagine happening to the protagonist under tension as the action reflects the world surrounding her now.

RECORD

Record the time you start writing: _____

Record the time you stop writing: _____

Total number of words you wrote today: _____

Daily writing goal is: _____

Projected ending date: _____

Energy level: _____

Plot your scene above or below the line on a Plot Planner or your own chart.

PROMPT 14

AFFIRMATION PROMPT

I am grateful for the ideas and inspiration that come to me when I write and even when I'm not thinking about my story. I consider new ideas in relationship to my vision of my overall story. The direction in which the protagonist is headed guides my story.

Today I write.

PLOT PROMPT

The establishment of the first goal at the beginning of the story launches the Dramatic Action Plot (for more discussion of this, see *The Plot Whisperer*, Chapter 3). The other goal settings keep the energy of the dramatic action plot moving higher and faster. Each time you make your protagonist's goal known to the audience, the energy swells.

WRITING PROMPT

Write a scene that re-establishes the protagonist's goal to the reader. Need an idea for the exact right setting or situation to thrust her in? Follow her goal and give the obvious a try.

Show the protagonist forced to move in a new and different direction because of the conflict in the scenes you wrote over the past couple of days.

RECORD

Record the time you start writing: _____

Record the time you stop writing: _____

Total number of words you wrote today: _____

Daily writing goal is: _____

Projected ending date: _____

Energy level: _____

Plot your scene above or below the line on a Plot Planner or your own chart.

PROMPT 15

AFFIRMATION PROMPT

I rewrite the stories I tell myself that best support my daily writing goal.
Today I write.

PLOT PROMPT

The beginning of your story establishes who the character is, flaws and all. Your readers can look back to this portrait and compare it to who she becomes as she undergoes a transformation after the crisis. This portrait also foreshadows who she will be at the climax.

WRITING PROMPT

Introduce a new character with her own set of goals, which may or may not be in direct conflict with the protagonist's goals, and who holds a key to the protagonist's overall growth later in your story.

Choose a setting that best supports the new character. Center the action on the new character as she moves forward with her goal. Close enough is perfect.

RECORD

Record the time you start writing: _____

Record the time you stop writing: _____

Total number of words you wrote today: _____

Daily writing goal is: _____

Projected ending date: _____

Energy level: _____

Plot your scene above or below the line on a Plot Planner or your own chart.

PROMPT 16

AFFIRMATION PROMPT

Following the rhythm of this ritual is changing me. I feel more confident in my writing and in my life. There is power in ritual, and I see it every day I continue.

Today I write.

PLOT PROMPT

As important as scene writing is, summary has its place in stories, too. In stories that span a long time or wide geography, one scene cannot always smoothly move into the next. To avoid the story becoming episodic, you must make creative use of summary. (Also, a story made up only of scenes can inject too much conflict and become exhausting for the reader.) Summary is a place to make transitions. Rather than play out every moment in scene, a summary compresses time and space.

Summary narrates quickly those events that are not important enough to the overall story line to show in detail. It helps move the story forward quickly. That way you, as the writer, can concentrate on creating scenes that show the most important moments in your plot.

WRITING PROMPT

Summarize routine behavior that moves the characters more quickly through time, by hours or days, weeks or months, or even years. Integrate the ideas the protagonist has about life and how life works around her.

As you write, imagine the protagonist at the end of the story. Consider the different ways in which her beliefs about life may change over the course of the story. With those ideas about the end of the story in mind, show who she is now and what she believes about life now; this will later appear in sharp contrast to who she is at the end.

RECORD

Record the time you start writing: _____

Record the time you stop writing: _____

Total number of words you wrote today: _____

Daily writing goal is: _____

Projected ending date: _____

Energy level: _____

Plot your scene above or below the line on a Plot Planner or your own chart.

PROMPT 17

AFFIRMATION PROMPT

My goal for today is to write. Nothing else I do today is as important as that.

Today I write.

PLOT PROMPT

When a task must be accomplished and a promise fulfilled within a defined period of time and for a specific purpose, the reader pays attention. The shorter the time frame and the greater the reward or punishment for completion, the more the reader is held by the narrative. A longer time frame with lesser reward or punishment still moves the story forward, but more slowly.

WRITING PROMPT

Show the protagonist accepting or resisting a task that must be accomplished and a promise that must be fulfilled within a defined period of time and for a specific purpose.

Show the protagonist's strength and how it will help her to accomplish this task. Write a memory the protagonist has or someone else has about the protagonist related to this strength. Explore how her strength ties the rest of the story together thematically.

RECORD

Record the time you start writing: _____

Record the time you stop writing: _____

Total number of words you wrote today: _____

Daily writing goal is: _____

Projected ending date: _____

Energy level: _____

Plot your scene above or below the line on a Plot Planner or your own chart.

PROMPT 18

AFFIRMATION PROMPT

A sense of expansion and growth fills me. My daily writing practice enriches my life. I marvel at the words I write today.

Today I write.

PLOT PROMPT

Characters have fears that derive from universal emotions. The protagonist's fears can be sparked by an external foe—anything from an irritable parent to a malfunctioning robot. Anytime that foe is mentioned or present, the energy of the scene surges and creates a sense of anticipation: *Will she survive or will she be crushed?* The more powerful the character, the more powerful the external force.

Other fears are divorced from any concrete and immediate danger and are about something that *could* happen. They create tension in the protagonist as she wonders when and how those internal fears will affect the action of the external story. Fear of failure, fear of being hurt, fear of making the wrong decision, fear of loss, fear of death—all these keep the protagonist disconnected from her true power. What she fears gives the reader insight into her emotional makeup and points to what she must ultimately confront in order to transform.

WRITING PROMPT

The protagonist takes what she believes are necessary steps toward the task she learned about in the previous writing prompt. Show the protagonist interacting with something or someone she loves, someone or something dependent on the successful completion of her task.

Create a scene with some sort of action, something that keeps it from being overly introspective and shows what scares your protagonist the most.

This time, rather than write the first idea that comes to you, wait for a moment. Allow the information to sink in, the obvious to appear, and then see if the idea that comes next isn't just a little bit less clichéd. Is it better, more unique and authentic to your story, and a little more tied thematically to the whole of the story and connected by cause and effect?

Give the reader insight into the protagonist's emotional makeup and point to what she must ultimately confront in order to transform.

RECORD

Record the time you start writing: _____

Record the time you stop writing: _____

Total number of words you wrote today: _____

Daily writing goal is: _____

Projected ending date: _____

Energy level: _____

Plot your scene above or below the line on a Plot Planner or your own chart.

PROMPT 19

AFFIRMATION PROMPT

I enjoy my daily writing. I feel motivated by the challenge of writing every day purely for the sake of creating a story from beginning to end.

Today I write.

PLOT PROMPT

The loss the protagonist will suffer if she is unsuccessful in reaching her goal determines what motivates her to strive for her goals, even in the face of tremendous odds. The greater the risk, the more exciting the story.

Some motivating forces are:

- Revenge
- Love or hate
- A promise
- Rebellion
- Betrayal
- Self-sacrifice
- Ambition

Motivating forces usually involve another character.

WRITING PROMPT

As you write, stay aware of the mood and promise of the story and convey them in scene. Show how the protagonist notices something new in her surroundings, something that has been there all along but that she only now notices. What surprises her about that?

Experiment writing one version of the scene as fast and violent, another version that is slow and moody, one that is angry and choppy, another sexy and brooding, and then one that is innocent and scary. Each time notice something new.

RECORD

Record the time you start writing: _____

Record the time you stop writing: _____

Total number of words you wrote today: _____

Daily writing goal is: _____

Projected ending date: _____

Energy level: _____

Plot your scene above or below the line on a Plot Planner or your own chart.

PROMPT 20

AFFIRMATION PROMPT

I take full responsibility for my writing. I depend on myself to make the time and take the time to write my daily word count.

Today I write.

PLOT PROMPT

Secondary characters' subplots create depth in a piece of writing when they tie into and support the development of the primary character. This development is better understood as the protagonist's Character Emotional Development (for more discussion of this, see *The Plot Whisperer*, Chapter 3).

Do not repeat the previous interactions between the protagonist and other main or secondary characters; instead, make the exchange more complex and give your reader a deeper understanding of the protagonist's emotional development.

This is true for all your characters. Each time one of them reappears, it should give the reader a deeper glimpse into the character—strengths, weaknesses, and all.

WRITING PROMPT

Introduce what another character—preferably a major or secondary character—wants, shown by the action that character takes in opposition to what the protagonist wants.

RECORD

Record the time you start writing: _____

Record the time you stop writing: _____

Total number of words you wrote today: _____

Daily writing goal is: _____

Projected ending date: _____

Energy level: _____

Plot your scene above or below the line on a Plot Planner or your own chart.

PROMPT 21

AFFIRMATION PROMPT

Every day I write, I improve at staying true to my writing goals and my writing commitment to myself.

Today I write.

PLOT PROMPT

A phrase, observation, or use of an object that is important to the story and introduced early, when revisited, lends thematic weight to the overall story. Repetition creates pattern recognition and provides significance. Reiterate the same detail again (although not always in the same words) and you establish rhythm.

A detail re-encountered from 100 pages earlier in the story reminds the reader and audience of a past experience. The feeling of a shared history with the story's protagonist creates a bond that resonates with readers and audiences long after the story has ended.

Do not take time now to develop all the significant details that will be necessary to inform and enhance all your scenes. However, one or more details that appear in the first draft, such as a sound, a color, a movement, or a location, become an opportunity to go back later and perfect the image, giving it a deeper meaning that emerges over time. Pinpoint those opportunities now.

WRITING PROMPT

Show the protagonist thwarted as she moves to fulfill the task in the required time period, while also showing the relationship the protagonist has with either an antagonist or an ally. Show restraint in what you "tell" about their relationship and/or the individual. Intimate drama or tension in their mutual backstory, if there is one, but do not elaborate . . . yet. (Save the best stuff for the middle.)

If this scene takes place in the same setting as a previous encounter between these two characters, be sure to show something substantially different about the protagonist that the reader did not learn in the earlier scene. Never repeat. Deepen.

Introduce a symbol, phrase, observation, or use of an object that is important to the story now, with the potential to be revisited later for thematic weight.

RECORD

Record the time you start writing: _____

Record the time you stop writing: _____

Total number of words you wrote today: _____

Daily writing goal is: _____

Projected ending date: _____

Energy level: _____

Plot your scene above or below the line on a Plot Planner or your own chart.

PROMPT 22

AFFIRMATION PROMPT

Every day I write. Every day I log in how many words I write. I enjoy watching the word count of my story grow daily.

Today I write.

PLOT PROMPT

The beginning of every great story reflects what comes at the end. This means you cannot determine what comes at the beginning until you know what happens at the end. T. S. Eliot said it best: "The end is in the beginning."

The beginning of any entertaining and well-crafted story foreshadows where the characters will be at the end. If you're going to successfully lay the groundwork for the character and show the plot building to a climax in a way that makes the crowning glory of the entire story seem both inevitable and surprising, you first need to know what happens at that climax. This means that *until you write the end, you do not truly know the beginning.*

WRITING PROMPT

Today, if you have even the vaguest inkling of the end of your story, write a scene that foreshadows what you imagine there. If the ending involves a gun, write a scene now that has a gun. If the ending involves violence, show violence in a scene now. If the ending involves a sense of justice, show a sense of justice, or lack of it, in a scene now. If the ending involves facing fear, write a scene now in which she faces a similar fear.

RECORD

Record the time you start writing: _____

Record the time you stop writing: _____

Total number of words you wrote today: _____

Daily writing goal is: _____

Projected ending date: _____

Energy level: _____

Plot your scene above or below the line on a Plot Planner or your own chart.

PROMPT 23

AFFIRMATION PROMPT

I write without judgment. My writing is neither good nor bad. I concentrate on putting words on the page every day and count myself successful each time I write.

Today I write.

PLOT PROMPT

The scenes in the beginning build from the beginning of the story to the end of life as the protagonist currently knows it. The story's beginning ends when some long-enduring, rigid mentality loosens its grip; at that moment the story shifts from the beginning into the middle.

WRITING PROMPT

Show the protagonist begin to find fault with her life and the way it's unfolding. Actions she accepted or enjoyed performing early in the story now fall flat, and she finds herself resisting them.

Show her emotions changing within the scene. This emotional change can build up incrementally over time and affect the overall story arc, but mostly her emotions are fleeting—from happy to sad, scared to angry, and so forth.

RECORD

Record the time you start writing: _____

Record the time you stop writing: _____

Total number of words you wrote today: _____

Daily writing goal is: _____

Projected ending date: _____

Energy level: _____

Plot your scene above or below the line on a Plot Planner or your own chart.

PROMPT 24

AFFIRMATION PROMPT

The daily ritual of affirmations, exploring plot, and writing is uncovering new sides of me. Every day, I improve at lining up my behavior and beliefs to match my goals.

Today I write.

PLOT PROMPT

Stories are structured as a series of real-time scenes. Watching a scene unfold on the page, we connect to the story. We walk in the shoes of a character and feel what she feels. Scenes in a story or novel create their own time and the sensation that the present moment is all that exists. Instead of merely reading the words, we sink into the story world and surrender our emotions to the illusion of the scene. Readers experience this time as the characters in the scene experience it.

This experience strengthens as we come to know the characters, care for them, and even worry about them. Our bodies respond on a visceral level; our hearts beat faster. We laugh and weep because we're involved in the story world so completely.

Writing in a combination of scene and summary varies the pace of the story and provides interest.

WRITING PROMPT

Today, in a combination of scene and summary, show the protagonist's reaction as the changes or conflict she feels around her intensify. Incorporate mood and metaphor, simile and description.

Try writing the same scene from a couple of different points of view, in a different setting, or with different symbols to inspire new ideas.

RECORD

Record the time you start writing: _____

Record the time you stop writing: _____

Total number of words you wrote today: _____

Daily writing goal is: _____

Projected ending date: _____

Energy level: _____

Plot your scene above or below the line on a Plot Planner or your own chart.

PROMPT 25

AFFIRMATION PROMPT

I release the desire to achieve something. I focus purely on the word count I'm writing in scenes today. I focus on putting words on the page.

Today I write.

PLOT PROMPT

Plot the subplots just as you do the primary plot. Move the action forward at a pace that matches the theme of your story. Plot out each step in each subplot along the way.

WRITING PROMPT

Show the romantic tension increase between the protagonist and her potential love interest. Make sure the encounter is true to both characters' emotional development plot.

The change between the two characters in the romantic plot can be in the form of the first kiss. If the romantic plot is represented as a friendship or partnership, some other intimate behavior will do—a handclasp, a gift, a message that bonds the two characters together.

✎ RECORD

Record the time you start writing: _____

Record the time you stop writing: _____

Total number of words you wrote today: _____

Daily writing goal is: _____

Projected ending date: _____

Energy level: _____

Plot your scene above or below the line on a Plot Planner or your own chart.

PROMPT 26

AFFIRMATION PROMPT

My plot and writing rituals connect me to the true miracle, a story uniquely my own.

Today I write.

PLOT PROMPT

Just as subplots complement the primary plot, every secondary character functions as a mirror, reflecting back to the protagonist the very elements she spots in others but is blind to in herself. Every secondary character, however minor, whether an antagonist, ally, friend, lover, or some combination, has something to teach, awaken, challenge, and love in the protagonist.

WRITING PROMPT

Introduce a new character or develop a previous character who is the complete opposite of the protagonist. Create in this character the very attributes the protagonist will need to embody in order to prevail at the end.

RECORD

Record the time you start writing: _____

Record the time you stop writing: _____

Daily writing goal is: _____

Projected ending date: _____

Energy level: _____

Plot your scene above or below the line on a Plot Planner or your own chart.

PROMPT 27

AFFIRMATION PROMPT

Every day I write, and every day I discover new gifts await me, invisible right up until the instant when words appear on the paper in front of me, as if by magic.

Today I write.

PLOT PROMPT

Rather than tell everything about the protagonist in the beginning, use the power of curiosity. Curiosity draws the reader deeper into the story world. Give away everything up front and you lose that.

WRITING PROMPT

A protagonist unable to do something creates in the reader a sense of curiosity about why: What caused her to be unable to do what she wants to do? What happened in the protagonist's earlier life?

Write a scene that shows signs of the protagonist becoming bored, restless, dissatisfied, anxious, or fearful about some element in her life and how the overall fixed world of her daily routine begins to constrict her.

Make sure you have introduced all the characters you believe will play an important role in the story. If you haven't already done this, do so now, even by merely mentioning them by name or showing them in passing.

RECORD

Record the time you start writing: _____

Record the time you stop writing: _____

Total number of words you wrote today: _____

Daily writing goal is: _____

Projected ending date: _____

Energy level: _____

Plot your scene above or below the line on a Plot Planner or your own chart.

PROMPT 28

AFFIRMATION PROMPT

Writing scenes demands present-moment attention. I enjoy the power I feel when I direct my full attention to writing each word on a page. That power begins now.

Today I write.

PLOT PROMPT

Every beginning uses certain techniques to draw the reader in further. Among the most important of these are contrast and foreshadowing, which work in tandem throughout the beginning of a story.

Every element introduced in the beginning provides a contrast for the middle and serves to foreshadow what comes later.

WRITING PROMPT

Today, in scene, show the protagonist stirred by an awakening desire or need for something different, something new.

RECORD

Record the time you start writing: _____

Record the time you stop writing: _____

Total number of words you wrote today: _____

Daily writing goal is: _____

Projected ending date: _____

Energy level: _____

Plot your scene above or below the line on a Plot Planner or your own chart.

PROMPT 29

AFFIRMATION PROMPT

Emotions inside of me intensify the more I write. I accept the drama. Throughout the roller coaster ride, every day I write.

Today I write.

PLOT PROMPT

Before the real drama and excitement of the story begins in the middle of a story, first the protagonist is forced to leave the physical, emotional, mental, and/or spiritual boundaries that make up the life she has always known.

Something or someone is the catalyst for forward movement that foreshadows the even greater change that comes later in the story. The character either consciously or unconsciously prepares for this first major change.

WRITING PROMPT

Today, write about someone or something, internal or external, whose action changes forever the protagonist's world. This may include someone important in the protagonist's life dying or leaving. The environment around the protagonist no longer brings her a sense of peace or joy. Show how what once was sharp and defined is now dull and gray, and yet incorporates the sense of impending change. Create this sense of a coming shift through the use of metaphor and/or symbolism to evoke a sense of separation from life as it was in the beginning of the story.

Show the character's preparations for or resistance to this new move so the reader can experience the changes herself.

RECORD

Record the time you start writing: _____

Record the time you stop writing: _____

Total number of words you wrote today: _____

Daily writing goal is: _____

Projected ending date: _____

Energy level: _____

Plot your scene above or below the line on a Plot Planner or your own chart.

PROMPT 30

AFFIRMATION PROMPT

I write the beginning of my novel, memoir, or screenplay. I enjoy writing to the end and finishing.

Today I write.

PLOT PROMPT

The beginning of a story lasts for about one quarter of the entire page or word count. The beginning of a story ends in a message to the reader that we're finished with introductions and ready to move on to the depths of the middle.

By now, you have written scenes showing what the protagonist wants and why. You have established her fears, flaws, and strengths to make her believable and to represent challenges she must overcome if she is to transform. You have lined up formidable antagonists, with goals in direct opposition to the protagonist's, who are ready to challenge her on her journey.

Now comes the time to catapult her into the very heart of the story world—the world of the middle.

WRITING PROMPT

Write about a threshold that separates the known world of the beginning from the unknown world of the middle of the story. Write about your protagonist crossing that threshold. More than where she is going, today write about the moment of leaving one reality for another.

Create dramatic anticipation of what comes next by slowing this moment of crossing without letting the reader know where she is going to end up. Tension and suspense are the result.

Show the protagonist willingly or unwillingly cross from the life you have written for her in the beginning into the unknown of the middle of the story. Show that there is no turning back, only forward into a new and unusual world.

End the scene (chapter) with a symbolic act or detail that alerts the reader that the protagonist is now at her destination, and that the beginning of the story is finished.

RECORD

Record the time you start writing: _____

Record the time you stop writing: _____

Total number of words you wrote today: _____

Daily writing goal is: _____

Projected ending date: _____

Energy level: _____

Plot the scene above the line on your Plot Planner and label it as the "End of the Beginning" scene.

PART II
THE HALFWAY POINT

The concepts used in this part's daily plot prompts support you in crafting the middle of your novel, memoir, or screenplay. The keynotes of the middle are resistance and struggle.

For more in-depth information about the plot elements used in this section, view the videos devoted to crafting the first part of the middle of a story on Martha Alderson's free YouTube channel. Read the sections about the essential plot considerations required in writing the middle in *The Plot Whisperer* (Chapter 9), *The Plot Whisperer Workbook* (Chapter 9), and *Blockbuster Plots: Pure & Simple*.

In this section, an important element is a special gift the protagonist has that is uniquely hers. Often it is a hidden ability of which she was robbed or that she surrendered or has forgotten. This secret skill could be a specific force that is to be revealed by her and her alone. Her unique gift has the power to heal herself and manifest her dreams.

PROMPT 31

AFFIRMATION PROMPT

Today I celebrate how far I have written in my story. Today I recommit to staying true to my writing goal.

Today I write.

PLOT PROMPT

The end of the beginning represents a break from the old world order as the main character embarks on a journey into an exotic new world. When the character enters the middle of the story, she is confronted with a new, strange, and challenging world that is fertile ground for expansion.

WRITING PROMPT

Write an opening scene for this section of the story; contrast the setting where the story started with where the action takes place now, be it a change in the protagonist's physical or mental environment or in her emotional landscape. Incorporate into the action a bird's-eye view of the place—an overview that shows a broad connection between the protagonist and her new setting.

Allow the reader to experience the new world moment-by-moment as the protagonist does, and through the protagonist's point of view; remember, she is entering the unknown.

Show her studying other people: what they're wearing, what they have to say, their mood. Shift her attention from herself to others.

Now that you're no longer in the introduction, find ways to deepen the reader's appreciation of who the protagonist is in a foreign world, challenged by unfamiliar obstacles.

RECORD

Record the time you start writing: _____

Record the time you stop writing: _____

Total number of words you wrote today: _____

Daily writing goal is: _____

Projected ending date: _____

Energy level: _____

Review the Character Emotional Development Profile for your protagonist. Assess how many traits and attributes of the protagonist you deepened in today's scene.

PROMPT 32

AFFIRMATION PROMPT

I am a great writer. Every day, I do what other great writers do.

Today I write.

PLOT PROMPT

Once you have an exotic world that stirs wonder, bewilderment, and even disorientation, deepen the reader's appreciation of the nuances of the unusual location, job, lifestyle, custom, ritual, sport, beliefs, state of mind, or whatever your imagination dreams up. The experiences the protagonist has in the new world will ultimately force her to reinterpret her belief system.

Take your time. In the way you shape the plot at this point, let us really see and experience where the protagonist and other characters are. Of course, include conflict, tension, suspense, and/or curiosity as well.

WRITING PROMPT

Advance the primary plot. Define the protagonist's goal as either the same as it's always been or something different now that her circumstances have altered.

Show her moving toward her goal, only to find that where she is now is greater, more complex, and more challenging than she first imagined.

Show the character displaying a range of emotions between passive engagement and aggressive aversion in reaction to the change in her environment.

Show how she notices everything, particularly the details.

RECORD

Record the time you start writing: _____

Record the time you stop writing: _____

Total number of words you wrote today: _____

Daily writing goal is: _____

Projected ending date: _____

Energy level: _____

Chart your scene above the Plot Planner line or your own chart if the protagonist is not in control of what is happening in her surroundings, and below the line if there is little to no conflict, tension, or suspense and the protagonist is in control.

PROMPT 33

AFFIRMATION PROMPT

Daily, I willingly release the urge to resist writing. Daily, I write.

Today I write.

PLOT PROMPT

When a character represents the sensibilities of her own country of origin, she provides her individual insight into the customs, beliefs, rules and regulations, politics, and reactions to them, based on her upbringing.

The country and politics of the story's physical location often take on features of actual characters and contribute to the entire picture of the story.

Build into your plot different views, be they abstract concepts such as nationalism and politics or other characters. This allows for a much bigger picture beyond the moment-by-moment scenes and links them into the psyche of the world around the characters. This adds a depth and richness to your story.

WRITING PROMPT

Show the protagonist react emotionally to the newness around her, using the sights, smells, tastes, textures, and sounds that best epitomize the new world.

Incorporate the nuances of setting, time frame, physical details, and dialogue. The only backstory information allowed is that which can be injected through word choices, mood, tone, actions, and reactions.

If appropriate to your story, incorporate history or politics to help broaden the overall scope of the tale. Show the protagonist work with what is in front of her while resisting the temptation to dwell on the past and what it is not.

RECORD

Record the time you start writing: _____

Record the time you stop writing: _____

Total number of words you wrote today: _____

Daily writing goal is: _____

Projected ending date: _____

Energy level: _____

Review the Character Emotional Development Profile for the antagonist. Assess how many traits and attributes of the antagonist you deepened in today's scene.

PROMPT 34

AFFIRMATION PROMPT

I am worthy of writing the very best story I know how to write. I lovingly allow myself to accept this knowledge and this challenge.

Today I write.

PLOT PROMPT

The more unusual the new world, surroundings, mindset, and demands of the middle of your story, the more exotic the experiences, explorations, endurance, and quest for survival will be. In the exotic new world, the old rules and beliefs no longer apply.

The protagonist is separated from all that is familiar. Her sense of self is shaken. Her attachment to learned attitudes and behavior is severed. The energy surge at the end of the beginning turned the story in a new direction. The protagonist enters into the actual story world with a goal that takes on greater meaning.

WRITING PROMPT

Throw a few strange, new-world challenges at the protagonist. Show the degree to which she struggles as she maneuvers in the new world. Let the readers experience this new world moment-by-moment as the characters in the scene experience it.

RECORD

Record the time you start writing: _____

Record the time you stop writing: _____

Total number of words you wrote today: _____

Daily writing goal is: _____

Projected ending date: _____

Energy level: _____

Plot your scene above or below the line on a Plot Planner or your own chart.

PROMPT 35

AFFIRMATION PROMPT

I approve of myself and of the way I am changing. The structure of my days revolves around my writing. I see others supporting my efforts and cheering me on.

Today I write.

PLOT PROMPT

Now that the protagonist is in the strange, new world, what keeps her going? Ask yourself:

- What does the protagonist most desire?
- What does she care about?
- What strongly motivates her?
- Toward what is the character actively moving?
- What keeps her going, focused, and committed when the going gets rough?
- What needs to be done, saved, protected, solved, fixed, achieved, figured out, or helped that she, and only she, can do?
- What is her plan to accomplish that?

WRITING PROMPT

Show an issue or situation in the protagonist's life that needs attention. Have her propose a course of action and then take the first step forward.

Integrate into the scene the answers to some of the questions above. Show the reader why the protagonist must go forward, though in her heart she may long to retreat.

RECORD

Record the time you start writing: _____

Record the time you stop writing: _____

Total number of words you wrote today: _____

Daily writing goal is: _____

Projected ending date: _____

Energy level: _____

Review the Character Emotional Development Profile for the protagonist. How have her goals and traits changed as you've been writing these prompts?

Plot your scene above or below the line on a Plot Planner or your own chart.

PROMPT 36

AFFIRMATION PROMPT

I am doing the best I can. Every day, showing up for my writing ritual gets easier.

Today I write.

PLOT PROMPT

What separates great books from good books is the degree to which an author is able to voice something only she and her unique truth can tell. The deeper meaning of your story and your life fills you with energy to write and live a more fulfilled life. The thematic significance statement reflects the truth of your story. This is not necessarily a universal truth, but it is true for your story.

WRITING PROMPT

List the themes with which your story deals so far. Ask yourself what those themes mean to you. What beliefs do you carry about those ideas? Are they consistent with what is expressed in your story? Watch for a pattern to begin to emerge.

Pinpoint a theme that truly resonates with you. Write a scene with that theme as your focus. Show your reader around the new and exotic world of the middle and give her the chance take in the new sights and sounds around her.

Show your protagonist resist what is happening to her. Show her fight the system—whatever that system is.

RECORD

Record the time you start writing: _____

Record the time you stop writing: _____

Total number of words you wrote today: _____

Daily writing goal is: _____

Projected ending date: _____

Energy level: _____

Plot your scene above or below the line on a Plot Planner or your own chart.

PROMPT 37

AFFIRMATION PROMPT

Daily, my writing flows. I rejoice that I am in the rhythm and spirit of my writing.

Today I write.

PLOT PROMPT

The ability to create tangible and concrete goals appropriate to the protagonist is critical to storytelling. Specific and concrete long-term goals create a dramatic question: Will she or won't she achieve her goal? Each time you make your protagonist's goal known to the audience, the energy swells.

A reader who knows what motivates the main character is able to closely connect and stay involved with the protagonist, and to calculate the progress the main character makes or doesn't make. The reader roots for her when she's successful and mourns when she is confronted with failure.

The steps she takes toward her goal create the dramatic action—the front story plot. Another core plot of your story revolves around your protagonist's inner development. To satisfy this inner plot, the protagonist must undergo a deep and fulfilling transformation, which often demands that she'll eventually have to face her main flaw and overcome it in order to achieve her ultimate goal. Though this doesn't happen until the end of the book, the middle is an important time to develop all the different ways in which the protagonist interferes with her own progress forward.

WRITING PROMPT

Re-establish what the protagonist's goal is now, both for the short-run and for the long-run, too. Write a scene that deepens how she trips herself up, using the strangeness of the new world around her as a factor in her failure.

RECORD

Record the time you start writing: _____

Record the time you stop writing: _____

Total number of words you wrote today: _____

Daily writing goal is: _____

Projected ending date: _____

Energy level: _____

Revisit the Character Emotional Development Profile for the protagonist. Plot your scene above or below the line on a Plot Planner or your own chart. Stay alert to how the protagonist's goals shift as the energy of the dramatic action swirls, while remaining true to her personal strengths and weaknesses.

PROMPT 38

AFFIRMATION PROMPT

Today is a writing day. I release old limitations—whether they be lack of confidence, concern for the quality of my work, or anything else that holds me back.

Today I write.

PLOT PROMPT

A character who fears something is vulnerable. A fear is something that has not happened yet, and a character's fear reveals what part of her is missing. What the protagonist fears most is precisely what she must face in order to transform and restore a sense of balance in her life.

WRITING PROMPT

Put the protagonist in the middle of what she most fears. An ally introduced at the beginning of the story arrives and is helpful to the protagonist.

There is meaning in everything the characters do. Explore the themes that circle around her fears and how she perceives the help offered to her.

RECORD

Record the time you start writing: _____

Record the time you stop writing: _____

Total number of words you wrote today: _____

Daily writing goal is: _____

Projected ending date: _____

Energy level: _____

Change the Character Emotional Development Profile for your protagonist to reflect what you're learning about your character.

Plot your scene above the line on a Plot Planner or your own chart. When the protagonist is under the spell of her flaw, she is always in conflict.

PROMPT 39

AFFIRMATION PROMPT

I am at peace with myself and with the process of writing a story from beginning to end.

Today I write.

PLOT PROMPT

A story is about a character transformed over time by dramatic action. The first quarter of the story shows a character within the safety of a world that is familiar to her. This gives the reader a starting point from which to evaluate the emotional change in the protagonist as, in the middle of the story, she is forced to break away and rely on herself.

In the middle, the protagonist can no longer act in her usual way because she is no longer in her usual life. Her inner protection from familiar customs, dogma, rules, and regulations is stripped away, making her vulnerable.

WRITING PROMPT

Today, begin a subplot between the protagonist and a secondary character like the ally or the love interest or some other character completely. Let the primary plot sink into the background for now, and let the subplot shine and help to develop the protagonist in a new way.

Write three scenes in this subplot that are tightly connected by cause and effect.

In the first scene, show the protagonist as she attempts to maneuver her way toward her goal, while keeping your eye on where she is going next.

Then, write a scene showing (in action) the effect of the first scene on how those around her in the world of the middle treat her. One scene creates the action in the next scene, and because of what happens in the second scene, you write the action in the third scene. Show what happens when the old-world set of beliefs, material goods, and behaviors from which she is having the most difficulty detaching assert themselves and try to drag her back.

Show as much contrast as possible between then and now: the environment the protagonist knew *then* versus the solitary, difficult, and dangerous new world she experiences *now*.

Show her questioning her purpose.

RECORD

Record the time you start writing: _____

Record the time you stop writing: _____

Total number of words you wrote today: _____

Daily writing goal is: _____

Projected ending date: _____

Energy level: _____

Plot your scene above or below the line on a Plot Planner or your own chart.

PROMPT 40

AFFIRMATION PROMPT

I stretch my body often during my writing time to stay limber and alert. I stretch my writing often to reach for new and unique angles and twists, descriptions and settings.

Today I write.

PLOT PROMPT

In every scene, the protagonist displays emotion in reaction to the dramatic action. How she reacts is often reflective of the burden she carries from her backstory. These emotions, which fluctuate within each scene, are usually transitory and fleeting.

The further the protagonist penetrates into the new and complex world, the more obstacles she confronts. Unable to function at a superficial level any longer, she begins to experience heightened emotions, ones that touch nearer and nearer to the core of her being. When she is prevented from reaching her goal, her emotional reaction changes subtly over time, flitting back and forth in each scene like a trapped fly.

The pattern of emotional change in the protagonist may be magnified or diminished based on the needs of each individual story, but emotion is always present and always communicates true feeling.

WRITING PROMPT

As you provide more sensory details about the landscape, the dress, the food, the language, the rules, and the customs of the new world around the protagonist, show her fleeting emotions that fluctuate according to the dramatic action around her.

Write a behavior using the nonverbal expressions of the emotions in the following list. Show the fluctuation in her feelings without telling how the character feels.

The following labels explore emotional expression:

- Exhausted
- Confused
- Ecstatic
- Guilty
- Suspicious
- Angry
- Hysterical
- Frustrated
- Sad
- Confident
- Embarrassed
- Happy
- Mischievous
- Disgusted
- Frightened
- Enraged

- Ashamed
- Cautious
- Smug
- Depressed
- Overwhelmed
- Hopeful
- Lonely
- Lovestruck
- Jealous
- Bored
- Surprised
- Anxious
- Shocked
- Shy
- Accepting
- Joyous

- Loving
- Averting
- Courageous
- Hateful
- Surprised
- Pleased
- Expectant
- Contemptuous
- Nervous
- Exasperated
- Elated
- Empowered
- Fearful
- Achieving
- Amused
- Satiated

RECORD

Record the time you start writing: _____

Record the time you stop writing: _____

Total number of words you wrote today: _____

Daily writing goal is: _____

Projected ending date: _____

Energy level: _____

Plot your scene above or below the line on a Plot Planner or your own chart.

PROMPT 41

AFFIRMATION PROMPT

I release my attachment to old belief patterns. I do not allow memories to interfere with my forward progress of writing words on the page. I allow memories to be . . . just memories.

Today I write.

PLOT PROMPT

Antagonists, because their role in stories is to prevent or delay the protagonist from successfully reaching her goal, always cause the energy of the story to rise.

Imagine a story as a conflict between forces of light and dark. The story shifts back and forth between the protagonist and the antagonists. The antagonists represent darkness, as they strive to keep the protagonist as she currently exists by darkening her path forward.

WRITING PROMPT

From all the characters introduced at the beginning of the story, write a scene that shows which character is now the most detrimental to the protagonist's progress.

Now that the protagonist has had time to orient herself in the new world, show actions between the protagonist in conflict with the antagonist, scenes that best epitomize the relationship between the two characters.

✍ RECORD

Record the time you start writing: _____

Record the time you stop writing: _____

Total number of words you wrote today: _____

Daily writing goal is: _____

Projected ending date: _____

Energy level: _____

Change the Character Emotional Development Profile you filled out for the antagonist to reflect what you're learning about that character as you write.

Plot your scene above the line on a Plot Planner or your own chart.

PROMPT 42

AFFIRMATION PROMPT

I forgive myself and release all my feelings of regret and sadness, hurt and fear, guilt and anger, resentment and revenge. I forgive all others, too. I write freely, unencumbered by the past.

Today I write.

PLOT PROMPT

Scenes in which an antagonist holds power over the protagonist create more energy than do scenes where the protagonist is safe and calm. Scenes in which the antagonist holds the power belong above the line in your Plot Planner. Plot the scenes in which the protagonist is in charge below the line. Scenes above the Plot Planner line keep the story moving. Scenes below the line slow the story.

An antagonist in the story doesn't have to consciously intend to hold back the protagonist's transformation. If asked, she might reply that her goal is simply to take her spouse out to dinner, give an employee a raise, or cleanse a believer of her sins. *The question is not about her intentions, but about their effect.* Whatever actions the antagonist takes or whatever feelings she inspires, the outcome initially will be to prevent the protagonist from reaching her goal.

Character flaws are often created and come to the surface in response to a loss of innocence, a loss that occurs before the story starts. The character stores the emotion generated by what happened in the backstory. In reaction—and mostly unconsciously—she often surrenders some or all of the authority over her own life to someone or something else.

WRITING PROMPT

Write a scene between the protagonist and an unwitting antagonist, someone or something that has no idea that what they are doing or saying is having a direct effect on limiting or squelching the protagonist's ability to move forward toward her goal.

Show the protagonist surrender some or all of the authority over her own life to the antagonist. Include her ally in the effect as the protagonist experiences yet another side of the exotic new world she is in.

RECORD

Record the time you start writing: _____

Record the time you stop writing: _____

Total number of words you wrote today: _____

Daily writing goal is: _____

Projected ending date: _____

Energy level: _____

Plot your scene above or below the line on a Plot Planner or your own chart.

PROMPT 43

AFFIRMATION PROMPT

Change is the natural flow of life. I embrace the changes I see around me: the changes in the choices I make to put my writing first and the changes in my attitude about my writing.

Today I write.

PLOT PROMPT

The reader experiences the protagonist's emotions on a visceral level as the protagonist finds her way. Employ as many antagonists as necessary to display a depth and breadth of emotions in your protagonist.

The tougher and cleverer the challenges and confrontations created by the antagonists, the greater the protagonist's eventual transformation will be.

WRITING PROMPT

Today, in scene, show an ally give the protagonist advice, help, insight, or a warning to better understand her feelings and this strange new world she's in.

✎ RECORD

Record the time you start writing: _____

Record the time you stop writing: _____

Total number of words you wrote today: _____

Daily writing goal is: _____

Projected ending date: _____

Energy level: _____

Plot your scene above or below the line on a Plot Planner or your own chart.

PROMPT 44

AFFIRMATION PROMPT

It is with joy that I learn more about plot and writing, and myself.

Today I write.

PLOT PROMPT

A character shows through her emotional reaction what she is thinking either consciously or unconsciously about what happens around her in the scene. The more identified she is with her thinking, her likes and dislikes, judgments and interpretation, the stronger her emotional reaction will be.

Hate is an intense emotion because it shows a darker side of the character and provides character complexity.

WRITING PROMPT

Today, in scene, show the protagonist interact with something or someone she hates.

RECORD

Record the time you start writing: _____

Record the time you stop writing: _____

Total number of words you wrote today: _____

Daily writing goal is: _____

Projected ending date: _____

Energy level: _____

Plot your scene above or below the line on a Plot Planner or your own chart.

PROMPT 45

AFFIRMATION PROMPT

I approve of my writing exactly as it is. I see my writing improve daily. Today I write.

PLOT PROMPT

In the beginning you spent a lot of time writing in scene because moment-by-moment action immediately engages a reader and pulls her deeper into the story. You also spent so much time in scene because you had many characters and themes to introduce to the reader. In the beginning you were given only a couple of opportunities to write in summary and practice compressing space and time.

WRITING PROMPT

In summary, write about the protagonist's review of her plan to achieve her goal and where she is in relationship to her goal. Show how near she thinks she is to success, how much time she has left, and her perception of the degree of difficulty she faces on the road ahead.

Show what she believes are or could be potential obstacles to her plan. (Foreshadow the obstacles you'll write about in scenes to follow, along with some unexpected twists.)

RECORD

Record the time you start writing: _____

Record the time you stop writing: _____

Total number of words you wrote today: _____

Daily writing goal is: _____

Projected ending date: _____

Energy level: _____

Plot your scene above or below the line on a Plot Planner or your own chart.

PROMPT 46

AFFIRMATION PROMPT

I choose to think about my writing in ways that nourish and support my will to write.

Today I write.

PLOT PROMPT

Adversity does not build character. It reveals what was already there.

Antagonists create adversity in order to reveal who the main character truly is. The deeper the protagonist travels into the middle of the story, the more conflict is thrust at her and the more nuances are revealed in her emotional development.

WRITING PROMPT

Immediately thrust the protagonist into step one of her plan. Show who is doing what, how the action is emotionally affecting the protagonist, and a general idea of where she is. In the first few drafts, ignore the specific details while you concentrate on how she deals with the anticipated or unanticipated obstacles she confronts.

Emphasize her flawed nature at this stage.

RECORD

Record the time you start writing: _____

Record the time you stop writing: _____

Total number of words you wrote today: _____

Daily writing goal is: _____

Projected ending date: _____

Energy level: _____

Plot your scene above or below the line on a Plot Planner or your own chart.

PROMPT 47

AFFIRMATION PROMPT

I release all opinions about my writing and the time I take to write. I honor the expression of my own individuality.

Today I write.

PLOT PROMPT

The greatest gift you can give a story is to allow the protagonist to fail or appear foolish, lonely, tedious, or ordinary. Until a character experiences failure, brokenness, fear, emptiness, and alienation, the alchemy of change cannot occur.

As your character is exposed to more and more peril and more and more unhappiness, she shows struggle and resistance. In doing so, she unknowingly and repeatedly surrenders her will to the antagonists.

WRITING PROMPT

As you show the protagonist struggle forward and demonstrate how her flaw hinders her progress, show how deep her flaw runs and foreshadow how ultimately devastating it could/will/might be.

RECORD

Record the time you start writing: _____

Record the time you stop writing: _____

Total number of words you wrote today: _____

Daily writing goal is: _____

Projected ending date: _____

Energy level: _____

Plot your scene above or below the line on a Plot Planner or your own chart.

PROMPT 48

AFFIRMATION PROMPT

I am meant to be me and to write this story.

Today I write.

PLOT PROMPT

The ability to increase the energetic intensity of your story demands that you become adept at developing clever obstacles and challenges for the protagonist. Each new obstacle is yet another opportunity to deepen the reader's understanding of all aspects of her personality and character development.

WRITING PROMPT

Write a scene in which the antagonist, an ally, or one of the secondary characters asks something important of the protagonist that goes against everything she has ever been taught. Show the actions having greater and more wide-ranging consequences than any of her previous challenges.

Show her flaw in a new light. Expand what her flaw looks like in all its forms.

 RECORD

Record the time you start writing: _____

Record the time you stop writing: _____

Total number of words you wrote today: _____

Daily writing goal is: _____

Projected ending date: _____

Energy level: _____

Plot your scene above or below the line on a Plot Planner or your own chart.

PROMPT 49

AFFIRMATION PROMPT

Slowly the uncertainty I often feel—the blind pursuit of my dream of holding this book—is replaced with confidence. Every day I write increases my confidence.

Today I write.

PLOT PROMPT

Secondary characters enhance the primary story and contribute to the meaning of the piece overall.

A secondary character goes after a goal. (Note: the more closely related thematically to the primary plot and the more at odds with the protagonist's inner plot, the better this goal will be; see previous prompt set.)

Other secondary characters are thwarted at every turn, which interferes with the protagonist's progress.

WRITING PROMPT

Explore and expand the interactions between one of the secondary characters and the protagonist as each of them pursues her own goals.

Show the secondary character taking action that thwarts the protagonist as she moves to fulfill her assigned task.

In the beginning, you showed restraint in what you told about the relationship between the two characters. Now reveal more of the drama and/or tension in their mutual backstory.

Incorporate a paragraph summary from the protagonist's point of view that gives a taste of her personal insight into their shared history and relationship.

RECORD

Record the time you start writing: _____

Record the time you stop writing: _____

Total number of words you wrote today: _____

Daily writing goal is: _____

Projected ending date: _____

Energy level: _____

Plot your scene above or below the line on a Plot Planner or your own chart.

PROMPT 50

AFFIRMATION PROMPT

I am in the process of positive change. Every day as I watch the word count for my novel or story grow, it fills me with confidence.

Today I write.

PLOT PROMPT

Abstractions and generalizations hold a story at surface level and keep readers at arm's length. Concrete and sensory details, on the other hand, penetrate to where emotion lies. They invite readers and audiences to think, to feel, and to actively participate in the story you tell.

Readers who believe you in the details will believe you in the bigger things to come.

WRITING PROMPT

Write about the part the protagonist will play in an upcoming social or political event, local custom, or ritual. Be specific as to details, including setting, sights, sounds, and smells.

RECORD

Record the time you start writing: _____

Record the time you stop writing: _____

Total number of words you wrote today: _____

Daily writing goal is: _____

Projected ending date: _____

Energy level: _____

Plot your scene above or below the line on a Plot Planner or your own chart.

PROMPT 51

AFFIRMATION PROMPT

Every day I write. As I do, I create my own future. Every day, I write toward a future of holding a completed book in my hands.

Today I write.

PLOT PROMPT

In the beginning you introduced a phrase, observation, or use of an object that is important to the story. When that element is revisited, it brings with it thematic weight. Repetition creates pattern recognition and provides significance. Repeat the same detail again and you establish rhythm.

A detail read 100 pages earlier in the story and repeated now reminds the reader and audience of a past experience. The feeling of a shared history with the story's protagonist creates a bond that resonates with readers and audiences long after the story has ended.

WRITING PROMPT

As the protagonist takes part in an event, show the knowledge and skills she gains. Incorporate an earlier phrase, observation, or use of an object that is important to the story, with differences stemming from the protagonist's insights into the setting, for thematic weight.

End the scene with an unexpected twist or setback.

RECORD

Record the time you start writing: _____

Record the time you stop writing: _____

Total number of words you wrote today: _____

Daily writing goal is: _____

Projected ending date: _____

Energy level: _____

Plot your scene above or below the line on a Plot Planner or your own chart.

PROMPT 52

AFFIRMATION PROMPT

I listen to the wisdom inside of me. When I write, I hear the silence of the universe.

Today I write.

PLOT PROMPT

The otherness of the new and exotic world manifests itself as differing cultures, personalities, ideas, value systems, landscapes, and languages.

The new world itself creates tension, conflict, and suspense merely by its unfamiliarity to the protagonist; thus, it produces a sense of overarching tension. In the new world, the old rules with which the protagonist is familiar and the beliefs she grew up with no longer apply.

WRITING PROMPT

Show something severe, dire, or extreme happen in the exotic world that is tied to an earlier scene. It should intensify the action and drastically interfere with the protagonist's forward movement.

Include a memory as it relates to the action in the scene.

RECORD

Record the time you start writing: _____

Record the time you stop writing: _____

Total number of words you wrote today: _____

Daily writing goal is: _____

Projected ending date: _____

Energy level: _____

Review the Character Emotional Development Profile for your protagonist. Revise and update it based on the knowledge and understanding of the character you've gained.

Plot your scene above or below the line on a Plot Planner or your own chart.

PROMPT 53

AFFIRMATION PROMPT

Every day an entirely new world opens up to me. I breathe in life's energy and breathe out creativity and passion. I give gratitude for the wonder of being here now and writing.

Today I write.

PLOT PROMPT

A real and tangible threat to the protagonist builds from what is an unusual setting in the beginning to the exotic world of the middle. An overarching threat of bodily, mental, or spiritual harm keeps the tension high and allows the story to slow down without losing readers' interest as scenes deepen the sense of place, time, and humanness.

WRITING PROMPT

Using what you wrote in the previous writing session, now create a sensation of or a reality of a tangible threat to the protagonist. Tie the character who most represents the romance plot into the action. Show the protagonist admitting love or appreciation for the character.

 RECORD

Record the time you start writing: _____

Record the time you stop writing: _____

Total number of words you wrote today: _____

Daily writing goal is: _____

Projected ending date: _____

Energy level: _____

Plot your scene above or below the line on a Plot Planner or your own chart.

PROMPT 54

AFFIRMATION PROMPT

I congratulate myself for the number of words I have written and how far I have come with my story. I know that my commitment is expressed by showing up and writing daily. I recommit to showing up and writing daily.

Today I write.

PLOT PROMPT

The deeper the protagonist wades into her story, the more emotional she feels—as do you. She examines, questions, and reacts to things she has always held dear. Having the beliefs she once identified with, which gave her a sense of herself, stripped away, she feels anger and frustration, disappointment and self-pity. She believes herself to be alone in her shame and self-loathing. She longs to run back to the safety of her life before things got so complicated.

WRITING PROMPT

Show the protagonist begin to doubt her ability to be creative, imaginative, willing, talented, disciplined, funny, and intelligent enough to actually accomplish her goal. As she falters, she wonders who she is without her old things, beliefs, and ideals.

Thematically link today's scene to the rest of the story through the actions of the character, the memories she has, the mood of the scene, and the metaphors used to connect one element to another.

RECORD

Record the time you start writing: _____

Record the time you stop writing: _____

Total number of words you wrote today: _____

Daily writing goal is: _____

Projected ending date: _____

Energy level: _____

Plot your scene above or below the line on a Plot Planner or your own chart.

PROMPT 55

AFFIRMATION PROMPT

My writing schedule is becoming a routine. I am aware of when I choose to write. I feel secure when I make time to write.

Today I write.

PLOT PROMPT

So far in your story, you know what your character wants and her reasons for wanting it. You have identified what only your protagonist can do, deliver, conquer, or overcome. The fears, flaws, and strengths you give her make her believable and represent challenges she must overcome if she is to transform. She has a gift, though she will have to go through trials and challenges to reclaim it. You know why this is her story.

You are aware of themes and details in your story. You strive for the physical and sensory details that help suspend reality and allow readers to fully involve themselves in the story's environment.

You have lined up formidable antagonists, each with goals in direct opposition to the protagonist's, ready to challenge her on her journey. You know where she has been and what her true journey and purpose are.

Soon you will write about the protagonist truly committing for the first time or recommitting to her goal and crossing the threshold into the second half of the middle.

Thresholds create suspense. Until the protagonist takes action, excitement grips the reader. Will she go forward as she planned, decided, or was persuaded to do? Or will she stay stuck? Or, through a plot twist, will she not go back to the old or forward to the expected, but instead turn somewhere else entirely?

WRITING PROMPT

Write a passage showing several antagonists appearing at once in the same scene, or in several separate but linked scenes. Create in the protagonist the sense of a formidable barrier blocking her forward progress.

Deepen the relationship the protagonist has with the antagonists. Reveal yet another layer about the individuals and/or their relationships.

RECORD

Record the time you start writing: _____

Record the time you stop writing: _____

Total number of words you wrote today: _____

Daily writing goal is: _____

Projected ending date: _____

Energy level: _____

Plot your scene above or below the line on a Plot Planner or your own chart.

PROMPT 56

AFFIRMATION PROMPT

I am serious about being the kind of writer who writes a story from the beginning to the end.

Today I write.

PLOT PROMPT

In order for the protagonist to prevail at the climax at the end of the book, she first must learn new skills, many of which may be present already but undiscovered, underdeveloped, or forgotten.

The challenges in the middle strip away her personal power, will, and autonomy. They tear apart beliefs, reveal judgments, and force self-confrontation, all of which serve the ultimate transformation at the end.

WRITING PROMPT

At the beginning of your story, you introduced a character who is the complete opposite of the protagonist and someone who embodies the very attributes the protagonist will need in order to prevail at the end. Show that character's advancement toward the successful completion of her goal, which opposes or is in conflict with what the protagonist wants. Show in a scene the ways in which the protagonist struggles in one direction against her opposing forces, which are determined that she move in another.

Write about how the protagonist begins to see cracks in her plan for success. Show her beginning to doubt herself.

RECORD

Record the time you start writing: _____

Record the time you stop writing: _____

Total number of words you wrote today: _____

Daily writing goal is: _____

Projected ending date: _____

Energy level: _____

Plot your scene above or below the line on a Plot Planner or your own chart.

PROMPT 57

AFFIRMATION PROMPT

Every day, I find the courage to begin writing. Every day, I find the courage to continue writing until I achieve my daily word count. Today, I have the courage.

Today I write.

PLOT PROMPT

Moving ever deeper into the exotic world, the protagonist begins to understand more of the rules of this new world and her place in it. If she looks back at the ordinary world, she feels guilt, regret, resentment, grievances, sadness, bitterness, and blame.

WRITING PROMPT

Remind the reader of the protagonist's goal, old or new, and where she is in relationship to her goal. Show how far she has come. Show her appreciation of all she has been through. Show how near or how far she thinks she is from success, how little time she has left, and her perception of how difficult the remaining portion of her task will be.

RECORD

Record the time you start writing: _____

Record the time you stop writing: _____

Total number of words you wrote today: _____

Daily writing goal is: _____

Projected ending date: _____

Energy level: _____

Plot your scene above or below the line on a Plot Planner or your own chart.

PROMPT 58

AFFIRMATION PROMPT

Daily, I cross from my normal, regular life over the threshold into my writing life and sacred space. Daily, I consciously turn my energy and focus to my writing.

Today I write.

PLOT PROMPT

As we have discussed, the middle of the story is the territory of the antagonists, which means that the antagonists control the new and unusual world. In this world, antagonists—internal and external—interfere with the protagonist's forward progress, creating tension and excitement. This back-and-forth between protagonist and antagonist forms the essential, dynamic Yin and Yang of stories.

WRITING PROMPT

Create a moment when the protagonist is given a hint, a sign, or an indication of what will be expected of her if she moves forward. This warning foreshadows what could happen to her at the crisis to come, the moment when she looks in the mirror and sees that she's lost her soul.

She takes action she believes is expected of her and will advance her own personal goals. The challenges mount. Show the protagonist's actions and how she reacts as life around her becomes more difficult.

Show her vision forward toward her goals dimming.

RECORD

Record the time you start writing: _____

Record the time you stop writing: _____

Total number of words you wrote today: _____

Daily writing goal is: _____

Projected ending date: _____

Energy level: _____

Plot your scene above or below the line on a Plot Planner or your own chart.

PROMPT 59

AFFIRMATION PROMPT

I greet the positive messages and the negative messages I give myself with equal acceptance and understanding.

Today I write.

PLOT PROMPT

As the energy rises and her defenses fall away, the main character opens up more and more to the reader. The more vulnerable she becomes, the more she reveals who she really is. Life gets harder, but little does she know just how much more difficult things are going to become.

WRITING PROMPT

Show another side of the protagonist. If she has been confident, show her stumble. If she's been in denial, show her alert. If she's been scared, show her courageous.

RECORD

Record the time you start writing: _____

Record the time you stop writing: _____

Total number of words you wrote today: _____

Daily writing goal is: _____

Projected ending date: _____

Energy level: _____

Plot your scene above or below the line on a Plot Planner or your own chart.

PROMPT 60

AFFIRMATION PROMPT

Today, I restate my writing goals. I commit to reaching the end of this draft of this book. The only way is forward.

Today I write.

PLOT PROMPT

The second major turning point in a story comes halfway through the story and forces the protagonist to willingly and consciously commit to the journey. Throughout all the drama in the middle, the Universal Story sends a bright and steady beacon of light. Exactly in the middle of the middle stands the second energetic marker. Reach it and recommit. When the protagonist most wants to run the other way, this is the precise moment for your protagonist and for you to forge ahead.

After recommitting to her goal(s) at the halfway point of the Universal Story (or for the reluctant hero, committing for the first time), the protagonist feels the energy in her life turn and rise in significance. This energetic surge is a warning to the reader: Wake up. Be alert. A crisis is coming.

WRITING PROMPT

Make clear to the reader what she is committing to. Show your protagonist on a teeter-totter, sliding between the fear of going forward into the unknown and the urge to go back and start again.

Faced with the potential of loss and failure, rather than give up, show her reconnect and recommit to her goal, her desire, her dream, and/or her love for another through the actions she takes.

RECORD

Record the time you start writing: _____

Record the time you stop writing: _____

Total number of words you wrote today: _____

Daily writing goal is: _____

Projected ending date: _____

Energy level: _____

Plot the scene above the line on your Plot Planner and label it as the "End of the Halfway Point" scene.

PART III
THE CRISIS

The concepts used in the daily prompts in "The Crisis" section of this book support you in crafting further into the middle of your novel, memoir, or screenplay. For more in-depth information about the concepts used in this section, view the videos devoted to crafting the second part of the middle of a story on Martha Alderson's free YouTube channel.

Read the sections about the crisis in *The Plot Whisperer* (Chapter 10), *The Plot Whisperer Workbook* (Chapter 10), and *Blockbuster Plots: Pure & Simple*.

Near the close of this section comes a death, literal or figurative. Begin imagining now: What is left in the protagonist's world that if stripped from her would send her to her knees? The more she suffers and loses at the crisis, the more powerful and transformative the moment.

A story always has a point. As you write deeper into your story, continually ask yourself what the story's purpose is right now. What is the protagonist's purpose? Look for meaning.

PROMPT 61

AFFIRMATION PROMPT

I see my story in book form. I see my book sitting on bookstore shelves next to other novels, memoirs, or screenplays. I write this story all the way to the end.

Today I write.

PLOT PROMPT

Every character wants something. Throughout the story, you (and your character) continually decide what she is willing to give up to achieve her goal. Each time she does give something up, it expands the character's emotional development plot.

The specific actions the character takes to realize her goal comprise the dramatic action plot.

Tie the character's private passion to a bigger, more transformative, universal subject and a thematic plot is launched. When the dramatic action changes the character over time, the story becomes thematically significant.

Rather than retreat, this is the time to crank up the energy. Now that the protagonist has adapted to the new world around her and survived, she knows she cannot fall prey to the mistaken belief that by making a commitment, the hard work is behind her. If she does, she will step forward into thin air and fall with a resounding thud.

WRITING PROMPT

Show your protagonist taking action toward her goal. Show off her talents and traits. She believes she is in control now that she is fully committed to the journey. She moves with confidence deeper into the story, no longer afraid of how she goes about ensuring her success. She is willing to use any and all strategies at her disposal as she makes what she thinks is the final push forward.

Use the everyday world of sense perceptions. Physical details in a scene evoke a sensory awareness in the reader. Connect more deeply into the story through the senses of sight, taste, hearing, touch, and smell.

If she has an object that retains a protective power or special meaning to her and helps to reinforce the overall thematic significance of your story, use it.

Everything in stories is a potential symbol for something else. Make metaphor, analogy, significant detail, and every word serve more than one purpose.

✎ RECORD

Record the time you start writing: _____

Record the time you stop writing: _____

Total number of words you wrote today: _____

Daily writing goal is: _____

Projected ending date: _____

Energy level: _____

Review the Character Emotional Development Profile for your protagonist. Assess how many traits and attributes of the protagonist you deepened in today's scene.

PROMPT 62

AFFIRMATION PROMPT

When I write daily, I feel it. My close family members also feel it. All my friends feel it, too. Not too much. Not too little. No interference. Every day I write.

Today I write.

PLOT PROMPT

By now, the reader has an idea of who all the major characters are, their emotional makeup, and the weight they carry in the story.

The middle of a story leading up to the crisis often has a subplot of its own. This subplot contains a beginning (as the character leaves her ordinary world and enters the exotic world) that leads to a middle. A rise in intensity often corresponds with the second energetic marker of the overall story's primary plot, when the protagonist commits to the journey. A subplot that lasts only as long as the middle culminates energetically just before the third energetic marker of the primary plot's crisis. (Do not confuse a crisis with the climax. The climax comes at the end of the overall story and shows the character fully in her own personal power. The crisis shows the protagonist at her worst—after all, it *is* a crisis.)

A major subplot in the middle is the antagonist's primary plot. Conflict, tension, suspense, urgency, and curiosity keep the reader turning the pages to learn what happens next in a story.

The deeper the protagonist travels into the middle of the story, the more nuances are revealed in her emotional development. If you have held back before, bring on the antagonists in the middle and thrust the protagonist into conflict. This will help you emphasize her flawed nature at this stage in her progress.

WRITING PROMPT

Show a shift and a rise in intensity in the relationship between the protagonist and the antagonist, with the antagonist taking on more power. Remember, make the action in this scene different than in all the earlier scenes between the two of them. Show them in back-and-forth action.

Teach us something about the protagonist and/or antagonist we don't already know. Deepen the dramatic action.

Show the antagonist taking on more power at each turn. The protagonist suffers. Finish with a cliffhanger.

RECORD

Record the time you start writing: _____

Record the time you stop writing: _____

Total number of words you wrote today: _____

Daily writing goal is: _____

Projected ending date: _____

Energy level: _____

Plot your scene above or below the line on a Plot Planner or your own chart.

PROMPT 63

AFFIRMATION PROMPT

Every day I sit down to write, I find my chaotic mind calms more quickly and a path opens to my writing. I feel balanced and eager for today's writing practice.

Today I write.

PLOT PROMPT

The protagonist embarks on a transformational journey, not to gain something new but to regain what was lost, as represented in the backstory. Scenes in the beginning show what the character is unable to do now due to flawed beliefs. Whether she is conscious of it or not, she is on a journey to relearn or re-attain a skill or knowledge that has been lost, forgotten, or stolen, something that is necessary for her to conquer her greatest challenge at the climax.

No longer ambivalent and having truly committed, she assumes her fate will improve, that her reward for recommitting is success, and that she is near to attaining her goal, only to find that things are about to get worse.

Powerful antagonists leap in, and she quickly finds herself under siege, pummeled by forces intent on preventing her success. The energy of the story fills with more conflict, tension, suspense, and/or curiosity.

WRITING PROMPT

Imagine what the protagonist does at the climax at the end of the book. Whatever skills, strengths, or powers she needs to prevail then, show them now as missing, rough, or forgotten in her.

As the energy rises and her defenses fall away, the character opens up more and more to the reader. The more vulnerable she becomes, show the protagonist reveal more of who she really is. Write a scene that shows how life is getting harder. Hint at just how much more difficult things are going to become.

If she has a backstory wound and you have held back on giving information about the past, now you can begin to show more. Show only enough to engage the reader's curiosity and draw her deeper into the story world to discover why the character acts as she does. (Full discovery does not happen until after the crisis.)

RECORD

Record the time you start writing: _____

Record the time you stop writing: _____

Total number of words you wrote today: _____

Daily writing goal is: _____

Projected ending date: _____

Energy level: _____

Review the Character Emotional Development Profile for the antagonist. Assess how many traits and attributes of the antagonist you deepened in today's scene.

PROMPT 64

AFFIRMATION PROMPT

I write that which pulls me in, captures my imagination, fills me with passion to write, and fires me up with energy.

Today I write.

PLOT PROMPT

The shifting of power back and forth between the protagonist and the antagonist now moves all the way to the antagonist's advantage and stays there. Self-doubt and uncertainty begin to smother the protagonist. She struggles with shortcomings. Yet she also discovers strengths she did not know she possessed.

Scenes within a chapter hold the same sort of structure as the overarching plot of a story: There is a beginning with steps toward a goal or desire, followed by some sort of conflict or tension and ending with a cliffhanger.

Ending a chapter with a cliffhanger, you keep curiosity high and create a page-turner book.

WRITING PROMPT

Show the protagonist struggle against the antagonist and for the first time seriously accept that she truly may lose. End the scene with a cliffhanger.

RECORD

Record the time you start writing: _____

Record the time you stop writing: _____

Total number of words you wrote today: _____

Daily writing goal is: _____

Projected ending date: _____

Energy level: _____

In most scenes with an antagonist, the antagonist is in control. If that is the case with your scene, plot your scene above the line on a Plot Planner or your own chart. If the protagonist is in control of what is happening, plot the scene below the line.

Usually scenes where the protagonist is in control have little to no conflict, tension, or suspense, unless she is threatened by an antagonist.

PROMPT 65

AFFIRMATION PROMPT

I find myself dreaming about my story. Writing soothes and calms me.

Today I write.

PLOT PROMPT

The new world deals in opposites—rapture and anguish, light and shadow, ego and unity, good and evil. Antagonists, both external and internal, emerge from every angle in the middle of the story. These obstacles can be human or nonhuman. Other challenges originate in the character herself, in other people's fears and judgments, and in the rules of society.

The protagonist becomes more and more conscious of her thoughts, feelings, and actions and sees her life differently. Any joy she experiences in success is best modulated—if she thinks her victory constitutes a sign that conquest is near, she quickly finds herself mistaken and it becomes incumbent upon her to re-evaluate the situation. No route forward is without its dangers and peril.

WRITING PROMPT

Immerse the protagonist in situations where she is not in control, where she is faced with her greatest fear and with what she most hates, treachery and opposition.

Rip all power from the protagonist and transfer it to the antagonist. Make the dramatic action a contest of searing intensity between the two. Threaten the protagonist with more tension and disruption. Put her under more strain and stress in each progressive scene. Show that the more she denies and becomes exasperated and overwhelmed, the greater her resistance and the more she struggles.

Introduce a time limit for her to complete a specific act, one that others may caution her against but she is convinced will move her ahead by leaps and bounds.

RECORD

Record the time you start writing: _____

Record the time you stop writing: _____

Total number of words you wrote today: _____

Daily writing goal is: _____

Projected ending date: _____

Energy level: _____

Review the Character Emotional Development Profile for the love interest character. Assess how many traits and attributes you showed of that character in today's scene.

Plot your scene above or below the line on a Plot Planner or your own chart.

PROMPT 66

AFFIRMATION PROMPT

The greatest gift I give myself is the courage to fail or to appear foolish, lonely, tedious, or ordinary. I write through all of it.

Today I write.

PLOT PROMPT

Not all antagonists are people. Nature itself can be a formidable antagonist —as monumental as a flood, a hurricane, or an earthquake. Nature as an antagonist can work on a more subtle level, too. Because the protagonist is powerless to control nature, she either resists or surrenders to it. Nature as an antagonist can create mood and add depth to the thematic significance of the conflict, tension, and suspense.

Rather than treat natural events as random occurrences in the plot, assign them deliberate meaning in each scene and in the overall story. Nature awakens primal emotions in both characters and readers. Take advantage of this.

WRITING PROMPT

Count down the time left until the protagonist reaches her deadline.

Show how something happens in the natural world around the protagonist that interferes with her forward progress. Show the effect the delay has on the protagonist.

RECORD

Record the time you start writing: _____

Record the time you stop writing: _____

Total number of words you wrote today: _____

Daily writing goal is: _____

Projected ending date: _____

Energy level: _____

Plot your scene above or below the line on a Plot Planner or your own chart.

PROMPT 67

AFFIRMATION PROMPT

Today, all is well in my world.

Today I write.

PLOT PROMPT

The protagonist grows alarmed and bewildered, angry and hateful, jealous and envious, fearful and sad. She exhibits these negative emotions as her confrontations with the antagonists become more vigorous and tumultuous. The character's flaws that were merely introduced earlier are revealed now in the full scope of dysfunction. If she was shown as controlling in the beginning, now when she is threatened, we see to what lengths she is willing to go in order to regain control. If she was shown as fearful, we now see how deep that fear runs.

WRITING PROMPT

As the energy of the story builds, the protagonist becomes painfully aware of an almost continuous undercurrent of low-level unease, restlessness, boredom, and nervousness. Show her as anxious, fearful of something looming and ready to strike. Her best behavior long gone, she passes judgments. Negative emotions grow within her. She resents, resists, and denies.

Show how much time has passed and where she is in relationship to the completion of her task, which she continues to be convinced will serve her interests well, even though she is met by obstacles every which way she turns.

RECORD

Record the time you start writing: _____

Record the time you stop writing: _____

Total number of words you wrote today: _____

Daily writing goal is: _____

Projected ending date: _____

Energy level: _____

Plot your scene above or below the line on a Plot Planner or your own chart.

PROMPT 68

AFFIRMATION PROMPT

I let go of all resistance. I move to the rhythm of creating something (a story) out of nothing (thin air). I reshape my life to allow for creative and productive growth that works for me as a writer. I allow myself to learn what I need to learn to make the next step easier.

Today I write.

PLOT PROMPT

Details shape the reader's attention and judgment. Every paragraph of your story has meaningful and memorable details that help establish the themes of your story.

Balance the use of details for emphasis. Do not overdo it; a scene can get buried in too much detail, obscuring the characters and the action. Report only the details that matter and are significant, and that reinforce the character(s), action(s), and theme(s) of your story.

Your protagonist moves two steps forward and falls one step back. Situations around her become more and more challenging.

Actions that show resistance

- Leaving the room
- Getting sick
- Procrastinating
- Looking away
- Looking out the window
- Creating breakdowns: cars, appliances, plumbing, etc.
- Changing the subject
- Eating, drinking, or smoking
- Creating or ending a relationship
- Being late
- Refusing to pay attention
- Flipping through a magazine

(This list comes from Louise Hay's book, *You Can Heal Your Life*, Chapter 6.)

WRITING PROMPT

Show your character dealing with a resistant antagonist. Write a scene that shows what the protagonist does when resisting something required of her and how those around her act in response.

Show time ticking away, adding more and more pressure to the protagonist.

✎ RECORD

Record the time you start writing: _____

Record the time you stop writing: _____

Total number of words you wrote today: _____

Daily writing goal is: _____

Projected ending date: _____

Energy level: _____

Change the Character Emotional Development Profile for your protagonist to reflect what you're learning about your character.

Plot your scene above the line on a Plot Planner. When the protagonist is under the control of her flaw, she is in conflict.

PROMPT 69

AFFIRMATION PROMPT

Writing shuts out the noise of my everyday life and balances me. I love to write.

Today I write.

PLOT PROMPT

Bad things happen to your characters in the middle of the story and especially during the crisis. They may be hurt, betrayed, or lost. They may become angry or vindictive. People may walk over them, pounce on them, or do other, more gruesome things. If you're in love with your characters, you'll instinctively be reluctant to let any of these things happen to them.

WRITING PROMPT

Put your protagonist in a horrible situation and show something really bad happen to her. Make this a big scene in which the protagonist and an outside forces collide. Consider what you want the confrontation to show on the human level and on the emotional level of the character's personal life.

Show that the battle is on. Quicken the pace. Raise the stakes and the story's intensity.

RECORD

Record the time you start writing: _____

Record the time you stop writing: _____

Total number of words you wrote today: _____

Daily writing goal is: _____

Projected ending date: _____

Energy level: _____

Plot your scene above or below the line on a Plot Planner or your own chart.

PROMPT 70

AFFIRMATION PROMPT

As I intensify the obstacles facing the protagonist and delve into her angst, I free myself of drama in my own life. I make choices that best serve my writing. I am calm.

Today I write.

PLOT PROMPT

As the protagonist moves deeper into the new world, emotions she has suppressed and therefore never processed begin to well up and unravel her self-control. She, of course, is not aware of how the antagonists mirror her own dysfunction. Instead, she sees imperfection only in others.

Unable to function at a superficial level any longer, she begins to truly *feel*. Intense emotions, usually negative, escape from beneath the surface. She reacts with anger, fear, aggression, and depression. She attacks, argues, judges, and blames with jealousy, wanting control. Often she withdraws, hostile and seeking revenge.

The more she is prevented from reaching her goal, the more emotions she experiences. Now, she not only has to acknowledge her feelings but actually *feel* them. Only then can she learn from her feelings and grow to trust them, and herself.

WRITING PROMPT

The horrible event to which the protagonist reacts sets off all her defenses and excuses. She tries to hide her head in the sand, talk her way out of problems, rationalize her failings, and blame others for her inadequacies.

She considers where she is in relationship to her goal. She specifies the short-term goals and the specific tasks, objectives, and actions she determines will take her nearer to accomplishing her long-term goal within a clearly defined period of time. Be clear about to whom and to what you direct your reader's attention in order to assist them in determining when to cheer and when to mourn for the protagonist.

RECORD

Record the time you start writing: _____

Record the time you stop writing: _____

Total number of words you wrote today: _____

Daily writing goal is: _____

Projected ending date: _____

Energy level: _____

Plot your scene above or below the line on a Plot Planner or your own chart.

PROMPT 71

AFFIRMATION PROMPT

The stillness of writing brings me a mental calm. I enjoy writing.

Today I write.

PLOT PROMPT

In the middle of the story, masks fall away and the characters reveal themselves—their flaws, fears, judgments, and all. Fights can ensue between characters . . . and between the characters and you. Feelings get hurt. The characters reveal their darker sides.

Action caused by an antagonist always creates conflict, tension, and suspense in the minds of your readers. Although they think they know how the protagonist will react, they are curious about what aspects the protagonist will reveal of herself. Antagonists, as we've said, operate as mirrors to the protagonist by revealing those parts of her that need to be healed.

The deeper the protagonist ventures into this new world, the more intense the energy of the dramatic action becomes, as the antagonists work more rigorously to block her forward movement.

WRITING PROMPT

Show the protagonist to be surprised by what she reveals about herself.

Tie what is revealed about the protagonist to the overall plot either directly or thematically.

Show that the time to complete her task is nearly up. What will it mean to her if she is not successful? Show how far back a failure now would send her.

RECORD

Record the time you start writing: _____

Record the time you stop writing: _____

Total number of words you wrote today: _____

Daily writing goal is: _____

Projected ending date: _____

Energy level: _____

Change the Character Emotional Development Profile you filled out for the antagonist to reflect what you're learning about that character as you write.

Plot your scene above the line on a Plot Planner or your own chart.

PROMPT 72

AFFIRMATION PROMPT

Writing makes me feel strong. I turn off the judge in my head and I write. I like to write.

Today I write.

PLOT PROMPT

The protagonist's flaw interferes with her attaining her goal—the very definition of an antagonist. In other words, *the protagonist acts as her own antagonist* each time she prevents herself from moving forward. This type of antagonist is especially powerful and connects viscerally with readers because many of us recognize how much we stand in the way of our own happiness.

A flawed character is more appealing to readers and moviegoers than is a character who is perfect. In the middle of a story, the character's emotional defenses begin to break down and her emotions turn bleaker and darker.

The secondary characters reflect lessons the protagonist needs to learn and the abilities she can most easily develop. A secondary character often reflects the natural and usually hidden abilities in the protagonist.

WRITING PROMPT

Show the protagonist become conscious of a lesson from another character or get a hint at the potential within her that she has forgotten, lost, or been robbed of. Show her, for the first time, wondering about why all this conflict is happening to her. Have her spot a part she plays in the drama around her.

Tie what the character learns to the primary plot.

RECORD

Record the time you start writing: _____

Record the time you stop writing: _____

Total number of words you wrote today: _____

Daily writing goal is: _____

Projected ending date: _____

Energy level: _____

Plot your scene above or below the line on a Plot Planner or your own chart.

PROMPT 73

AFFIRMATION PROMPT

An inner wisdom quietly nourishes my writing. Writing nourishes me.
Today I write.

PLOT PROMPT

The progression of the protagonist's internal flaw or character emotional development plot often serves as a subplot to a dramatic, action-driven story, in which the primary plot revolves around external action. The dramatic action demands a goal. The character's emotional development demands growth.

The protagonist's internal conflict or fatal flaw reveals what she needs to achieve internally in order to gain the goal of the primary plot. The resolution of the primary plot is dependent upon the resolution of the internal subplot. Before she can change her flaw, she must first become conscious of what she is doing and of the effect she has on others and herself.

WRITING PROMPT

Show the protagonist becoming more and more conscious of what she is doing and of the effect she has on others and herself. Show her taking a tried-and-true action in which she found strength and success at the beginning of the story. Show her emotional reaction when, this time, her foolproof strategy falls flat and dies.

Show her reach her time limit without having accomplished the task.

RECORD

Record the time you start writing: _____

Record the time you stop writing: _____

Total number of words you wrote today: _____

Daily writing goal is: _____

Projected ending date: _____

Energy level: _____

Plot your scene above or below the line on a Plot Planner or your own chart.

PROMPT 74

AFFIRMATION PROMPT

Reading these prompts connects me to my own internal flow of feelings. I listen.

Today I write.

PLOT PROMPT

The first three items on the character profile establish the Dramatic Action Plot:

1. Goals provide motivation.
2. Obstacles create tension.
3. Potential loss promises transformation.

In order to achieve her long-term goal, the protagonist must act and meet antagonists head-on. This is what creates the drama of the plot. (For more on the Dramatic Action Plot, see *The Plot Whisperer*, Chapter 3.)

WRITING PROMPT

Show the protagonist with an ally and what the protagonist still needs to learn about herself or, more to the point, needs to *relearn* and become conscious of in order to prevail at the end of the story.

✎ RECORD

Record the time you start writing: _____

Record the time you stop writing: _____

Total number of words you wrote today: _____

Daily writing goal is: _____

Projected ending date: _____

Energy level: _____

Plot your scene above or below the line on a Plot Planner or your own chart.

PROMPT 75

AFFIRMATION PROMPT

I win back my true self every time I write.

Today I write.

PLOT PROMPT

Summary makes the time pass and history unfold quickly. Keep in mind, however, that summary, no matter how well written, ultimately distances the audience from the character and the immediacy of the story. Summary is a place to fill in any missing gaps in your story.

A crisis is looming. Get the protagonist in place.

WRITING PROMPT

Move the story ahead with a summary of minor events that clears the way to a pivotal scene.

RECORD

Record the time you start writing: _____

Record the time you stop writing: _____

Total number of words you wrote today: _____

Daily writing goal is: _____

Projected ending date: _____

Energy level: _____

Plot your scene above or below the line on a Plot Planner or your own chart.

PROMPT 76

AFFIRMATION PROMPT

I pay attention to my breathing when I write. Not too much. Not too little. I do not push. I do not pull. I follow my breath and I write.

Today I write.

PLOT PROMPT

More aspects of the story's themes are revealed in the middle.

Character flaws are often created by a loss of innocence—often traumatic. This loss occurs before the story starts. It's even possible that the character may be unaware of this loss, either because she did not know it when it occurred or because she has repressed the memory. Nonetheless, the memory is there, no matter how deeply buried. The character stores the emotion created by what happened in the back-story. In reaction, she often surrenders some or all of the authority over her own life to someone or something else.

WRITING PROMPT

Show the protagonist take a risk in pursuit of her goal. Consider all the scenes you've written in the exotic world. How many different locations does she travel to? Ask yourself, why that particular location for that particular action? Expand your imagination.

As she moves forward and is confronted by antagonists, show her resist, either passively or aggressively, the antagonist's interference. Depict her using a new tactic, hoping it will prove to be a shortcut to her goal. Show a couple of different ways in which the strategy backfires.

✍ RECORD

Record the time you start writing: _____

Record the time you stop writing: _____

Total number of words you wrote today: _____

Daily writing goal is: _____

Projected ending date: _____

Energy level: _____

Plot your scene above or below the line on a Plot Planner or your own chart.

PROMPT 77

AFFIRMATION PROMPT

I make my breath longer and smoother, calmer and quieter. My words join together and are no longer separate. I join together with my destiny every time I write.

Today I write.

PLOT PROMPT

The character takes a step toward a goal or desire. The scene's moment-by-moment action creates conflict and tension as shown through dialogue, facial expressions, gestures, and every detail of the character's response. The scene ends with failure, an unanswered question, a cliffhanger, or a mishap that entices the audience deeper into the story.

All along and especially throughout the middle, the story is building to a crisis. The reader tastes it, senses it, and feels it coming. She tries to pretend nothing bad is about to happen, but there is no denying the inevitable. Doom is about to strike. There is no other place for the story to go.

On some level, the character knows it, too. Emotions intensify as the energy of the story rises.

WRITING PROMPT

Write a light scene where the protagonist achieves one of her short-term goals.

Show her stick out her neck, make a mistake, and then blame someone else or hide her part in the mistake.

Though she is successful, let her experience a sense of doom and a threat to her well-being.

✍ RECORD

Record the time you start writing: _____

Record the time you stop writing: _____

Total number of words you wrote today: _____

Daily writing goal is: _____

Projected ending date: _____

Energy level: _____

Plot your scene above or below the line on a Plot Planner or your own chart.

PROMPT 78

AFFIRMATION PROMPT

Every day I write new words. These words become my story. All is well in my world.

Today I write.

PLOT PROMPT

The protagonist is nearly at the center of the new and complex world. Gatekeepers intensify their guard of the passage both ways. In classical mythology, the gateway to the Underworld was guarded by Cerberus, a fierce three-headed dog.

Sometimes the challenge is not a physical guardian, but a barrier presented inside the character. Each time the protagonist is prevented from reaching her goal, she experiences heightened emotions that touch nearer to the core of her being.

WRITING PROMPT

Rather than move the character to another location, give the protagonist a task of solving a problem where she is, using only the materials at hand.

Show how she holds her body, the tone of her voice, the message she speaks, and the actions she takes as the challenge grows more difficult. Offer clues about her emotional response to the action or dialogue around her. Show her emotions through her actions.

Keep her emotions and her actions true to the character you introduced at the beginning of the story.

RECORD

Record the time you start writing: _____

Record the time you stop writing: _____

Total number of words you wrote today: _____

Daily writing goal is: _____

Projected ending date: _____

Energy level: _____

Plot your scene above or below the line on a Plot Planner or your own chart.

PROMPT 79

AFFIRMATION PROMPT

I focus my mind on my breathing. My breathing connects me to my story.

Today I write.

PLOT PROMPT

Things get messy as the relationships between the characters develop. Scenes show the characters and the demands of their relationships as they truly are—warts and all. For writers who like things nice and neat, the middle, especially in the buildup to the crisis and the crisis itself, is an uncomfortable place to linger for very long.

The essence of writing in scene is action.

WRITING PROMPT

Write a gritty scene in which someone you introduced earlier is threatened, hurt, or affected negatively because of the protagonist's flaw or shortcomings. No matter how desperate she is to avoid the awful truth of what is soon going to strike, she focuses on what comes next and keeps moving forward.

 RECORD

Record the time you start writing: _____

Record the time you stop writing: _____

Total number of words you wrote today: _____

Daily writing goal is: _____

Projected ending date: _____

Energy level: _____

Plot your scene above or below the line on a Plot Planner or your own chart.

PROMPT 80

AFFIRMATION PROMPT

I write every moment of my story as new, fresh, and vital.
   Today I write.

PLOT PROMPT

Each scene in the middle shows who the character is on a progressively deeper level. This means you have to subject your protagonist to tougher and tougher challenges. The energy throughout the middle is more intense than in the beginning, as the protagonist is more rigorously blocked from reaching her goals.

WRITING PROMPT

Show the protagonist fail again due to her flawed personality.

RECORD

Record the time you start writing: _____

Record the time you stop writing: _____

Total number of words you wrote today: _____

Daily writing goal is: _____

Projected ending date: _____

Energy level: _____

Plot your scene above or below the line on a Plot Planner or your own chart.

PROMPT 81

AFFIRMATION PROMPT

I relinquish control of my writing. I surrender to the plot ideas I learn today. I stay alert and energized. I write what needs to be written. Today I let the words flow.

Today I write.

PLOT PROMPT

The story moves from scene to scene through cause and effect. Conflict in a scene represents the motivating cause that sets a series of events in motion. The character's reaction to those events represents the effect the conflict has on the character. The character responds to the conflict. That response becomes the cause of the next action, which produces another effect.

Each time the character succeeds or fails as she goes after her specific goals, show her emotional reaction to this success or failure. Every part plays into the whole, and you end up with a satisfying story.

WRITING PROMPT

Show the major antagonist's progress toward her goal—the crisis looming for the protagonist is where the antagonist prevails. The protagonist's crisis will be the antagonist's climax and crowning glory.

Show the antagonist take steps that make her more and more successful and, at the same time, diminish the protagonist. Remember, an antagonist is any internal or external force that interferes with the protagonist reaching her goals.

RECORD

Record the time you start writing: _____

Record the time you stop writing: _____

Total number of words you wrote today: _____

Daily writing goal is: _____

Projected ending date: _____

Energy level: _____

Plot your scene above or below the line on a Plot Planner or your own chart.

PROMPT 82

AFFIRMATION PROMPT

I deserve to write a novel from beginning to end. I deserve to be a writer. I write now.

Today I write.

PLOT PROMPT

The protagonist of a story is the character most changed by the dramatic action. All other characters and the setting(s) influence the protagonist's journey toward her goal directly, indirectly, or thematically. The growth and transformation of the protagonist is the line that runs through the entire plot.

Think of the protagonist's crisis as the antagonist's climax, where the antagonist prevails and the protagonist fails. The protagonist is only as good as her antagonists.

Throughout the entire beginning and middle of a story, antagonists are always more powerful than the protagonist and seem to always find just the right buttons to push to bring out the worst in the protagonist.

The height of the antagonist's power comes at the crisis, when the protagonist is confronted by a moment of truth; thereafter, nothing is ever the same.

WRITING PROMPT

Write the world of your story in symbolic terms. Use mood, metaphors, analogies, and descriptions for meaning and for the greatest good of the story.

As you write, challenge the underlying assumptions your story makes. Out of a vast array of possibilities, you choose to weave certain ideas and concepts into the fabric of your protagonist.

Now change the imaginary lines in which you have boxed her. Write that.

RECORD

Record the time you start writing: _____

Record the time you stop writing: _____

Total number of words you wrote today: _____

Daily writing goal is: _____

Projected ending date: _____

Energy level: _____

Plot your scene above or below the line on a Plot Planner or your own chart.

PROMPT 83

AFFIRMATION PROMPT

I surrender to the flow of writing. The words come effortlessly.

Today I write.

PLOT PROMPT

A character flaw is a coping mechanism that arises from the loss of an original state of perfection that occurred in the character's backstory. Her flaw is designed to compensate for a perceived vulnerability, sense of insecurity, and feeling of being threatened. No matter how confident, every major character demonstrates lessons learned from the wound inflicted in her backstory, a flaw that is now lodged in her core belief system.

WRITING PROMPT

Show the protagonist's flaw cracking apart. Do not tell why or the details about her backstory wound (that comes later). For now, show how her defense mechanisms begin to let her down, fail her, malfunction, and foreshadow the doom to come at the crisis.

The protagonist may begin to suspect the part she plays in her failures and problems, but rather than face up to *herself* when confronted with problems, she points to the faults and flaws of others and blames them, while denying and ignoring her own issues.

✎ RECORD

Record the time you start writing: _____

Record the time you stop writing: _____

Total number of words you wrote today: _____

Daily writing goal is: _____

Projected ending date: _____

Energy level: _____

Plot your scene above or below the line on a Plot Planner or your own chart.

PROMPT 84

AFFIRMATION PROMPT

I am in the process of positive change. The more words I write, the better I feel.

Today I write.

PLOT PROMPT

The crisis that is coming is an energetic surge in your story, powerful enough to turn the dramatic action in a new direction, creating a whole new level of intensity and contributing to your story's thematic significance.

The degree of violence and explosiveness is in direct proportion to the story's mood that you've established. A suspenseful, high-action, thrilling story demands high intensity. A dramatic-action story releases quite a bit more obvious physical energy than does a quieter, slower, and more internal character-driven story.

Whether the crisis represents an emotional or circumstantial upheaval in the character's life, it releases the reader's fatigue and frustration and creates unbearable tension for the character and the reader.

WRITING PROMPT

Think of your story now as energy that is rising to the crisis. Guide the energy and direct the flow of your scenes to encourage the energy to crest and build for the greatest reader anticipation and emotional impact.

Write two or three scenes in quick succession that show the protagonist under more and more pressure as she is confronted by more and more adversity.

RECORD

Record the time you start writing: _____

Record the time you stop writing: _____

Total number of words you wrote today: _____

Daily writing goal is: _____

Projected ending date: _____

Energy level: _____

Plot your scene above or below the line on a Plot Planner or your own chart.

PROMPT 85

AFFIRMATION PROMPT

The practice of writing in scene becomes a spiritual rite. In the moments I write in scene, I live in the power of now.

Today I write.

PLOT PROMPT

Scenes ripe for emotional expression by the protagonist occur just before each energetic marker, and directly after it. One scene prepares and sets up the anticipation of something coming. A follow-up scene shows the full impact of the event on the character—both physically and emotionally.

Keep this sequence in mind:

1. Preparation and anticipation
2. Energetic marker and main event
3. Reaction and follow-through

Preparation and anticipation create emotion. Often your imagination makes a feared event worse in your mind than the actual event turns out to be. Preparation and anticipation generate tension, conflict, and suspense.

The protagonist is going to suffer a crisis soon, the greatest struggle of the entire story so far.

Scenes play out in the *now*. Evoke a true and authentically emotional moment and you have yourself a scene. The main character's flaw sets up the overall character arc and points to the potential for growth or transformation. Her flaw interferes with achieving her goal. It's dramatically great when the protagonist's own weaknesses cause, worsen, or create the coming crisis.

WRITING PROMPT

Show in a scene that the protagonist believes she is moving nearer and nearer to her long-term goal and consequent success. At the same time, infuse your writing with tension and conflict. Build the sense of the forces of impending doom converging toward a single point.

Show the results of each step she takes, making it clear when she is successful and when she fails so that the reader knows when to cheer and when to mourn.

RECORD

Record the time you start writing: _____

Record the time you stop writing: _____

Total number of words you wrote today: _____

Daily writing goal is: _____

Projected ending date: _____

Energy level: _____

Plot your scene above or below the line on a Plot Planner or your own chart.

PROMPT 86

AFFIRMATION PROMPT

Today is a new day. I am a new me. I write differently. I act differently.
I see myself differently. I see myself writing.

Today I write.

PLOT PROMPT

A disaster, catastrophe, emergency, calamity, major predicament, or crisis of any kind qualifies as the protagonist's darkest hour. She'll experience failure, brokenness, fear, emptiness, alienation, or a great loss . . .
but that crisis will reveal her true road. An emotionally significant event
or radical change of status in the protagonist's life leads, figuratively, to
death. Death leads the way to re-creation.

The crisis is the point in a sequence of scenes where the trend of all
future events, for better or for worse, is determined. It takes on dramatic proportions when it serves as the highest point in the dramatic
action plot line so far. The crisis is a key turning point in your story.

Before the crisis itself, tension and conflict steadily rise to the breaking point. The volcano erupts, or the river overflows. When the crisis
hits, the protagonist is traumatized.

The crisis is the lowest point in the entire story for the protagonist. At
the same time, it is a breakdown with the potential for a breakthrough.

WRITING PROMPT

Show hostile forces reach the tensest point of opposition. The protagonist moves toward her long-term goal and then receives information
that tears her further from what she wants. Separated, stretched too
far, held too tightly, or allowed too little, by herself, by others, by her
circumstances, or all of the above, the protagonist reaches her limit.

Show her fail and be duped, knocked out, ripped off, hurt, aban-
doned, or rejected. Because of her flaw, she puts everyone else around
her, those she cares about, and herself at risk of pain and disappointment, and even death.

Show her lose everything.

RECORD

Record the time you start writing: _____

Record the time you stop writing: _____

Total number of words you wrote today: _____

Daily writing goal is: _____

Projected ending date: _____

Energy level: _____

Plot your scene above or below the line on a Plot Planner or your own chart.

PROMPT 87

AFFIRMATION PROMPT

I deserve the best. I accept the best now.

Today I write.

PLOT PROMPT

The protagonist's world shatters. Only out of the ashes of the old self can a new self arise—the beginning of the character's ultimate transformation.

The crisis shakes things up in such a way that the protagonist *must* act.

WRITING PROMPT

The sudden release of energy in the crisis knocks the protagonist to her knees.

She is stunned by what is happening to her and is surrounded in darkness. Show her forced to confront herself and struggle to come to terms with who she is: her faults and her strengths.

Because of what happens when she fails, the protagonist begins to understand that she has been hiding from her faults and that her failure came in part or all because of her flawed thinking, behavior, and beliefs.

 RECORD

Record the time you start writing: _____

Record the time you stop writing: _____

Total number of words you wrote today: _____

Daily writing goal is: _____

Projected ending date: _____

Energy level: _____

Plot your scene above or below the line on a Plot Planner or your own chart.

PROMPT 88

AFFIRMATION PROMPT

I am doing the best I can. Every day I write.

Today I write.

PLOT PROMPT

The protagonist must overcome her flaw and release the consequent flood of emotion in order for her character to transform and the story to end.

The major challenge, threat, or loss in the protagonist's life situation (whether real or imagined), or the conflict in a relationship that was written as the crisis, causes a complete rupture between who the protagonist has always been and who she is destined to be. The tear comes from deep within her and symbolizes the cracking apart of her past identity.

A character flaw introduced in the beginning quarter of the story deepens as the energy of the story expands in the middle half. More and more often, the protagonist trips up. Now, she no longer can deny her own part in her failure. This newfound awareness brings about her ultimate transformation in the last quarter of the story.

Now, at last, the protagonist becomes conscious of who she truly is. In that new awareness, her old self dies and a new self is born.

She is forced to rethink life and herself. This wake-up call in turn changes her Character Emotional Development Profile. When one scene impacts both action and emotional plot lines in such a dramatic way, the scene acquires a lot of power and importance. This effect can generally be found toward the end of the middle or nearly three quarters of the way through the project.

WRITING PROMPT

The protagonist fails and appears tedious, foolish, ordinary, or lonely. As she surveys the damage around her, show her come to an understanding about the part she played in her failure, brokenness, fear, emptiness, and alienation.

She begins to understand that her real self is not who she has been all along. Show her commit to discovering her true, authentic self.

✍ RECORD

Record the time you start writing: _____

Record the time you stop writing: _____

Total number of words you wrote today: _____

Daily writing goal is: _____

Projected ending date: _____

Energy level: _____

Plot your scene above or below the line on a Plot Planner or your own chart.

PROMPT 89

AFFIRMATION PROMPT

I enjoy the exercise of writing words on the page every day. I give thanks for the words that appear.

Today I write.

PLOT PROMPT

The external action at the crisis destroyed all routes back to the familiar ground upon which the protagonist previously stood. The crisis changes her and—this is extremely important—*thus destroys all roads leading forward.* The protagonist is now trapped; both the way back and the path forward are closed. The only choice open to her is to change who she is at her core. Only by doing this will she find her way.

After the crisis, the energy of the story turns down briefly, and then expands. The pieces of the story begin to form a bigger picture.

Your protagonist's flaws do not come out of the blue. They usually originate in reaction to something in her backstory. Look for a memory that has stayed with her, lodged in her psyche in as much detail as the moment it first occurred. This memory does not have to be something huge. Often those big issues have been dealt with over the years. Frequently, it is the smaller events that are more profound. Perhaps on the surface her backstory moment is seemingly benign, but it has affected in a negative way how she views the world.

To dig for the cause of the situation in which she now finds herself, the protagonist must begin to understand what choices brought her here. This examination will offer clues about what to do next.

In a purely action-driven story, the protagonist's analysis is at the dramatic action level, as she looks only at external events and their consequences. In a character-driven story, the protagonist takes into account her own emotional development at each step along the way. As I hope you realize by this point, a combination of these two styles of writing—action-driven and character-driven; right-brained and left-brained—works best.

WRITING PROMPT

Your protagonist is offered the successful completion of her goal: the man or woman, the job, the answer to her burning question, peace, separation, security, success. In light of all she has been through, now the prize isn't as shiny and bright nor does it bring her as much happiness as she had imagined.

If you have resisted giving the reader a full understanding of the protagonist's backstory and especially her backstory wound, now is the time to open up and deliver the full backstory. Reveal what in the past made the protagonist lose her balance, creating the character she is today.

RECORD

Record the time you start writing: _____

Record the time you stop writing: _____

Total number of words you wrote today: _____

Daily writing goal is: _____

Projected ending date: _____

Energy level: _____

Plot your scene above or below the line on a Plot Planner or your own chart.

PROMPT 90

AFFIRMATION PROMPT

I appreciate the words that come to me. Inspiration, visions, and ideas connect me to my writing.

Today I write.

PLOT PROMPT

By slowing the action and drama after the crisis, when the energy rises to announce the final quarter, the story moves quickly and with maximum impact to the end.

Now is a time of perfect balance. Something has happened and something will happen. Only this exact moment is real.

The crisis serves as a slap in the face, a wake-up call, the moment when the character becomes aware of life's deeper meaning. Life takes the protagonist by the shoulders and shakes her until she sees life and herself as they both really are. The crisis jolts the character into a new acceptance, one in which transformation flourishes.

Throughout the story, the protagonist faces many obstacles. By far, the crisis is the worst. She survives, perhaps just barely. Now comes the time for her strength to kick in. She's going to have to pull herself up to get to the end. Her determination contributes to the forward movement of the story, because every time she is knocked down, she has the strength to get back up and continue toward her goal.

WRITING PROMPT

Because of what happens at the crisis, the protagonist finally sees the part she plays in her own failure. She acknowledges that she is the root of her own problems. The crisis awakens her to full consciousness and begins the process of moving toward acceptance and ultimate wisdom. Now you're ready to write this scene.

Show her learning to let go, detach, surrender, do things differently, get control of her life, and believe in herself.

Show her pull herself up and estimate what is necessary for ultimate success in achieving her goal. She gathers the attributes, things, and people to take forward with her on the final journey to the end.

Show her determination to persevere.

RECORD

Record the time you start writing: _____

Record the time you stop writing: _____

Total number of words you wrote today: _____

Daily writing goal is: _____

Projected ending date: _____

Energy level: _____

Plot the scene above the line on your Plot Planner and label it as the "End of the Crisis" scene.

PART IV

THE CLIMAX AND RESOLUTION

The concepts used in the daily plot prompts in "The Climax and Resolution" support you in crafting the end of your novel, memoir, or screenplay. Transformation and return are the keynotes of the end of a story.

For more in-depth information about the concepts used in this section, view the videos devoted to crafting the end of a story on Martha Alderson's free YouTube channel. Read the sections about the end in *The Plot Whisperer* (Chapters 11 and 12), *The Plot Whisperer Workbook* (Chapter 12), and *Blockbuster Plots: Pure & Simple*.

As you follow the prompts for the end, keep in mind where your character is going, what she believes she needs to confront in order to be complete or to make up for what happened at the crisis, and that one thing she's been waiting to do her entire life. Identify the special skills and knowledge she needs to succeed at the climax.

The answers come like wisps of vapor: one minute a brilliant idea comes to you; the next it's vanished. The further you delve into the prompts here, the more solidified your ideas will become. As you think of great challenges to throw at the protagonist as she marches steadily toward her greatest fear and foe at the climax, use them.

Throughout your daily writing sessions, search for clues for the exact, right, and appropriate climax and ending to your story.

PROMPT 91

AFFIRMATION PROMPT

Thanks to my determination and the ritual of daily showing up here, I am now ready to write the last quarter of my story. I willingly follow my story that daily pulls me forward. I breathe and remind myself to relax.

Today I write.

PLOT PROMPT

In contrast to the slowdown in the action and drama after the crisis, now the energy rises to announce the final quarter of the story. From here on out, it moves quickly and with maximum impact to the end.

The end begins when the protagonist leaves behind everything that does not serve the highest good and takes the first step necessary toward the completion of her long-term goal. Stories and lives demand action. One conscious outward movement symbolizes the closing of one door and the opening of another. In that step forward, the protagonist's life expands.

At their core, stories are about character transformation. Every movement forward signifies transformation has begun.

Whether the threshold to the next step is open and invites discovery or is closed, thresholds signify a space of perfect balance. Something has happened and something will happen. Only this moment is real. A threshold is a point of truth.

WRITING PROMPT

Emphasize the moment when the fully conscious protagonist takes the first step toward the completion of her final goal and the true ending of the story begins.

Show her emotional anticipation of the moment of crossing, the emotional and physical sensations of crossing over the threshold as it happens, and her reaction when the action is complete and the character understands she has entered the true belly of the beast.

Make it clear what her goals are now.

RECORD

Record the time you start writing: _____

Record the time you stop writing: _____

Total number of words you wrote today: _____

Daily writing goal is: _____

Projected ending date: _____

Energy level: _____

Review the Character Emotional Development Profile for your protagonist. Assess how many traits and attributes you showed of the protagonist in today's scene.

PROMPT 92

AFFIRMATION PROMPT

I practice writing every day. Every day, I take time to write.

Today I write.

PLOT PROMPT

The final quarter of the book shows the protagonist's ultimate regeneration from brokenness, fear, and alienation. Her rebirth is shown by the actions she takes to achieve her goal. Her changed behavior at the end of the story, compared to the way she acts at the beginning of the story, serves as proof that a transformation has occurred.

One sign of transformation is that now when the protagonist surrenders some or all of the authority over her own life to someone or something else, she is aware that she's doing so. Now when she gives up her power, she knows it—the beginning of true consciousness.

WRITING PROMPT

Show the protagonist immediately tested by a threshold guardian who tries to lure her back, away from what she most desires. As she hesitates before continuing into the great unknown, show her surrender, as usual, some or all of the authority over her own life to someone or something else.

As you did with the scenes in the beginning of your story, provide only enough of her plan forward to inform this particular scene. The reader is emotionally invested in the story when she wonders what will happen next.

RECORD

Record the time you start writing: _____

Record the time you stop writing: _____

Total number of words you wrote today: _____

Daily writing goal is: _____

Projected ending date: _____

Energy level: _____

Chart your scene above the line on a Plot Planner or your own chart if the protagonist is not in control of what is happening in her surroundings, or below the line if there is little to no conflict, tension, or suspense and the protagonist is in control.

PROMPT 93

AFFIRMATION PROMPT

This is one of the best days of my life.

Today I write.

PLOT PROMPT

Our range of emotions, including love, compassion, confidence, hope, despair, hate, envy, and fear, narrows as we grow into adulthood and are challenged to generate within ourselves an emotional steadiness. What particularly narrows is the range of emotions we permit ourselves to show others.

When your protagonist reaches obstacles in her story, note how she feels and how those inner feelings manifest themselves in her internal and external behavior. Use your findings to help inform your story's emotional weight.

WRITING PROMPT

As the protagonist considers the thoughts that have held her captive, she can mourn what was. But rather than hold on to those same old beliefs and continue to retard her progress, show her setting aside her old personality and reshaping her life by speaking and acting according to her own truth. Show her developing a new belief system, clearing herself to seize that which she most longs for.

The protagonist is still bombarded by her antagonists. To become whole and true, she attempts to balance those negative forces with an equal and opposite force—the positive.

Create dramatic action that is designed to get the protagonist to the right place at the right time to seize her personal power back from the antagonist, in a way that best represents the thematic significance of the entire story.

RECORD

Record the time you start writing: _____

Record the time you stop writing: _____

Total number of words you wrote today: _____

Daily writing goal is: _____

Projected ending date: _____

Energy level: _____

Review the Character Emotional Development Profile for the antagonist. Assess how many traits and attributes you showed of the antagonist in today's scene.

PROMPT 94

AFFIRMATION PROMPT

I write daily as a shining example of what one looks like when stepping forward in pursuit of her dreams.

Today I write.

PLOT PROMPT

The protagonist's reality is now developing around a set of new values, structures, and choices. No longer controlled by desires, external forces, and instincts of the past, she surveys resources, finances, values, emotional desires, possessions, addictions, and relationships. She works with intuition until she has gained a new perspective above, below, and on all sides of her life.

Now shifted from the material, external world of the ego to a more internal, compassionate focus, she is aware of the influence her backstory has had on her current status. She understands how the crisis or pain in her backstory created core beliefs about life itself, beliefs she now understands are flawed and without value in light of all she has been through.

She understands that no matter what experiences she has had in the world to convince her otherwise, she is a light at the center of the universe. The reader senses an alert stillness within the character. Along with renewed enthusiasm comes a new wave of creative energy.

WRITING PROMPT

Show the effect on those around her as the protagonist abandons old emotional ideas that no longer serve her. Show how the horizon in front of her broadens and intensifies. She both physically and intuitively sees the bigger picture of her life and the world around her.

RECORD

Record the time you start writing: _____

Record the time you stop writing: _____

Total number of words you wrote today: _____.

Daily writing goal is: _____

Projected ending date: _____

Energy level: _____

In most scenes with an antagonist, the antagonist is in control. If that is the case with your scene, plot your scene above the line on a Plot Planner or your own chart. If the protagonist is in control of what is happening, plot the scene below the line.

Usually scenes where the protagonist is in control have little to no conflict, tension, or suspense unless threatened by an antagonist.

PROMPT 95

AFFIRMATION PROMPT

I want to finish. I show my commitment to how much I want this by reading this affirmation. Today I write toward finishing.

Today I write.

PLOT PROMPT

Throughout the story, the protagonist's flaw has thwarted her quest for what she desires. Conflict, tension, suspense, and curiosity in the form of physical, psychological, and spiritual challenges or ordeals have created not only page-turning dramatic action; they have challenged the character with possible failure, or even death.

Facing failure and fear demands courage and faith. Each new and challenging situation forces self-confrontation.

WRITING PROMPT

Write two scenes in quick succession that are tightly connected by cause and effect. Show the protagonist see her greatest antagonist in a new light in one scene. In the next scene, show the effect of the previous scene as a new angle, idea, or resource comes to her for success.

Write a series of three scenes where questioning and discoveries in one scene lead characters to action in a second scene that reveals inner patterns and releases them from negative emotions, followed by a third scene showing the protagonist overcoming a shortcoming and developing a strength.

RECORD

Record the time you start writing: _____

Record the time you stop writing: _____

Total number of words you wrote today: _____

Daily writing goal is: _____

Projected ending date: _____

Energy level: _____

Review the Character Emotional Development Profile for the love interest character. Assess how many traits and attributes you showed of that character in today's scene.

Plot your scene above or below the line on a Plot Planner or your own chart.

PROMPT 96

AFFIRMATION PROMPT

Daily, I adjust my ideas for my story to align with the reality of what the story itself is becoming. Daily, I surrender my desire for how I'd like my story to be or thought it would be. Instead, I allow it simply to unfold.

Today I write.

PLOT PROMPT

Now that the protagonist has penetrated the heart of the new and complex world and survived all the obstacles, the heightened emotions she experiences are real.

How the protagonist holds her body, the tone of her voice, the message she speaks, and the actions she takes reflect her emotional maturity in response to the action or dialogue around her.

WRITING PROMPT

Show the protagonist able to adjust her behavior and control her emotions as conditions require. Show her challenged in action toward her goal. This time, rather than surrender some or all of the authority over her own life to someone or something else, for the first time, she consciously holds her ground and her own power.

✎ RECORD

Record the time you start writing: _____

Record the time you stop writing: _____

Total number of words you wrote today: _____

Daily writing goal is: _____

Projected ending date: _____

Energy level: _____

Plot your scene above or below the line on a Plot Planner or your own chart.

PROMPT 97

AFFIRMATION PROMPT

I let everything go of everything tangible and intangible and write.
Every day I write, I move nearer to the person I am.

Today I write.

PLOT PROMPT

Dreams or desires add yet another layer to a story. Dreams generally
rely on the help of others or a bit of magic and thus create an added
twist at the end of the story.

The linkage between the protagonist's goals and her dreams brings
thematic significance to your entire story and determines how you will
write each scene: word choices in dialogue, tone of voice, facial expression, body language, music, food, textiles, aromas, and physical objects.

The most original details convey your character's emotional reactions
to the dramatic action in the story. As you come to learn more about
the thematic significance of your story, the details become more specific
and unique to the story and, at the same time, achingly universal.

WRITING PROMPT

Show the protagonist take a similar action to that which she took in the
beginning or the middle of the story. This time, show how she performs
the same action in light of all she has learned about herself and her
relationship with others.

With the focus of the action toward the protagonist's push forward,
also use this opportunity to transform her imagined dream, which you
planted in the beginning of the book, into a real possibility.

RECORD

Record the time you start writing: _____

Record the time you stop writing: _____

Total number of words you wrote today: _____

Daily writing goal is: _____

Projected ending date: _____

Energy level: _____

Plot your scene above or below the line on a Plot Planner or your own chart.

PROMPT 98

AFFIRMATION PROMPT

Whatever I need comes to me. All is well.

Today I write.

PLOT PROMPT

Consider and develop the nuance of words and phrases, the atmosphere, and a sense of mystery, irony, humor, symbolism, satire, mood, rhythm, presence, timeliness, beauty, and/or harmony. Details authors use convey a fresh way of understanding the character's sensibilities and peel away the superficial to evoke the profound.

The details in scenes in the beginning quarter of a story bring into sharp focus the objects the protagonist most identifies with. These objects often reflect how she has been conditioned by her environment, upbringing, and culture and determine whether she goes into the new world of the middle as a willing adventurer or resistant and full of pain caused by the loss of these objects.

When the protagonist moves out of the ordinary and conditioned world into an exotic and unknown world, the details shift to reflect who she is as she journeys into the great unknown.

The details she surrounds herself with now, in the last quarter of the story, and especially at the resolution, reveal the character's truth. Details—hers and hers alone—deepen the reader's understanding of who the character is now and reflect her ultimate transformation.

WRITING PROMPT

Show a change from how the protagonist acted in the beginning and in the middle through a change in her choices and in her emotional responses, as a response to dramatic action.

Show her begin to recognize some of her own natural abilities. She wonders where they have been hiding, though in reality, they also feel as familiar to her as her own heartbeat.

Show her inner life and how the changes in her emotionally affect her.

In the context of the bigger picture of your vision, use details that expand thematic meaning.

RECORD

Record the time you start writing: _____

Record the time you stop writing: _____

Total number of words you wrote today: _____

Daily writing goal is: _____

Projected ending date: _____

Energy level: _____

Change the Character Emotional Development Profile for your protagonist to reflect what you're learning about your character.

Plot your scene above or below the line on a Plot Planner or your own chart.

PROMPT 99

AFFIRMATION PROMPT

When I think back over the sequencing of my earlier scenes, I am aware of mistakes and omissions, gaps and missteps in my story. I make note of the errors. I refocus on what I am about to write today.

Today I write.

PLOT PROMPT

Hate is a powerful negative emotion. When caught up in it, the protagonist is never in control of the emotion; rather, it controls her. This is true whether what she hates is external—another person, a job, a situation—or internal—her choices, her thoughts, her beliefs.

WRITING PROMPT

The threat of what the protagonist hates hovers nearby. She knows this emotion has to be faced. Show her directly confront that which she most hates; this is the moment when she relinquishes judgment, prejudice, and hatred.

RECORD

Record the time you start writing: _____

Record the time you stop writing: _____

Total number of words you wrote today: _____

Daily writing goal is: _____

Projected ending date: _____

Energy level: _____

Plot your scene above or below the line on a Plot Planner or your own chart.

PROMPT 100

AFFIRMATION PROMPT

There is always enough time. Time enough to write. Time enough to enjoy writing.

Today I write.

PLOT PROMPT

At the end of the story, every moment now breathes with anticipation of the crowning glory of the entire story: the climax.

The protagonist *must* do that which she has been putting off for her entire life. With a new sense of responsibility to herself, she finds value as she builds new attitudes and sensibilities and plans a new life for herself.

The fun of writing the end is that you get to remake the protagonist in whatever image you choose. In clichéd roles, behaviors, and choices, you show what already is. In inspirational roles, you show the way forward, what will be.

WRITING PROMPT

Create a scene in which the protagonist finds she does not want the prize that represents her old personality. She defines what she wants now.

Show her begin to use her special ability, gift, knowledge, or experience and quickly find that achieving what she wants is not as difficult as she once experienced.

RECORD

Record the time you start writing: _____

Record the time you stop writing: _____

Total number of words you wrote today: _____

Daily writing goal is: _____

Projected ending date: _____

Energy level: _____

Plot your scene above or below the line on a Plot Planner or your own chart.

PROMPT 101

AFFIRMATION PROMPT

Every day, I keep in mind the basics and then push off in a totally new direction, my own unique direction. Every day, I write.

Today I write.

PLOT PROMPT

Always express emotion through the character's body or voice. Tone, volume, facial expressions, and body language are universally recognized signals of emotion.

Nonverbal communication expresses emotion.

WRITING PROMPT

Write a scene showing the protagonist conscious of reinventing herself. She knows what she wants to take with her as she enters the future. Show her continue to readjust her attitudes and values, as well as which relationships she keeps and which ones she leaves behind.

She is no longer afraid to be herself, no longer afraid of failing or not being accepted, approved of, or liked. She looks back on her life and sees someone alien compared to who she is now.

No longer afraid, she spots an opportunity when it appears.

She puts her things in order and prepares for what she knows is coming.

RECORD

Record the time you start writing: _____

Record the time you stop writing: _____

Total number of words you wrote today: _____

Daily writing goal is: _____

Projected ending date: _____

Energy level: _____

Change the Character Emotional Development Profile you filled out for the antagonist to reflect what you're learning about that character as you write.

Plot your scene above or below the line on a Plot Planner or your own chart.

PROMPT 102

AFFIRMATION PROMPT

I gently take breaths that are longer, smoother, calmer, and quieter, until my words seem to join together with my breath and my breath and my words are one.

Today I write.

PLOT PROMPT

Now that her life is at its most challenging, your protagonist becomes receptive to guidance she would not have welcomed earlier. She becomes aware, perhaps for the first time, of disturbing emotions and impulses within her and what they lead her to do. She learns what creates stress for her and what motivates her best performance.

She identifies nonverbal clues in how others feel and begins to develop empathy. She considers new ways to listen, talk, and act that resolve conflicts instead of escalating them and develops strategies to negotiate for win-win solutions.

WRITING PROMPT

The protagonist finds that as she behaves in the manner most natural to her and trusts her innate abilities, her life begins to work.

She earns a clue into how to listen, talk, and act in a new, more productive way. Show her using this new information to her advantage.

RECORD

Record the time you start writing: _____

Record the time you stop writing: _____

Total number of words you wrote today: _____

Daily writing goal is: _____

Projected ending date: _____

Energy level: _____

Plot your scene above or below the line on a Plot Planner or your own chart.

PROMPT 103

AFFIRMATION PROMPT

A small amount of high-energy, good-quality practice is more beneficial than a lot of low-energy, poor-quality practice. I write every day with the highest energy for the greatest quality.

Today I write.

PLOT PROMPT

Now that she is consciously alert, the protagonist takes in more of the sensory details around her.

She knows from the crisis not to think her troubles have ended. Of all the previous challenges, nothing compares to the one that now beckons her at the end of the book. She fully expects her pain to grow worse before it gets better.

WRITING PROMPT

As you write, note the concrete details and thematic ideas you use. In light of all you know about the themes of your story, choose details, metaphors, and descriptions that reflect the thematic significance of the overall story.

Choose just the right words for just the right details that enhance the mood of the scene.

Remember back to earlier scenes you've written that involve another character teaching the protagonist a new behavior, tool, or idea. Now she extracts the lesson, reshapes the information to serve her needs right now, and synthesizes something new that works for her as a transformed individual.

RECORD

Record the time you start writing: _____

Record the time you stop writing: _____

Total number of words you wrote today: _____

Daily writing goal is: _____

Projected ending date: _____

Energy level: _____

Plot your scene above or below the line on a Plot Planner or your own chart.

PROMPT 104

AFFIRMATION PROMPT

I see my work as perfect. Every day I sit down to write, I improve my writing. Every time I look deeper into the structure of my story, I see an even more meaningful perfection awaiting me.

Today I write.

PLOT PROMPT

The buildup to the climax is a sequence of scenes that sets up the crowning glory of the entire story. In these scenes, the protagonist reclaims the power she previously relinquished to other people, places, and things. She responds to external conflict with actions and behaviors that show her breaking free from the patterns she has exhibited in the past. She takes action that shows she is moving toward who she was born to be.

The protagonist willingly, honestly, and accurately names her own culpability. Confronted with a potentially life-threatening and/or ego-threatening situation, she sees herself for who she is—flaws and strengths alike.

Stretch the space of this critical time just before the climax to build the suspense of the story. Suspense engages the reader. The protagonist is approaching her greatest fear, her greatest foe. Every step she takes narrows the time between one symbolic place and another. That the character is transitioning into the final test and the book is nearly over creates excitement, expectancy, and an element of fear of the unknown in both the character and the reader.

A story is about a character transforming her weaknesses into strengths.

WRITING PROMPT

Even knowing the magnitude of the final confrontation that awaits her, show the protagonist take action toward accomplishing all she intends to do. Show how her actions align with her belief in living a different life. Show her learning to use her natural abilities more effectively.

Empowered by the knowledge gained at the crisis, she now understands the rules of the life she has chosen to enter. Show her wiser and more powerful than she has been anywhere else in the story.

Show the antagonists grow in ferocity, too. Intensify the challenges.

RECORD

Record the time you start writing: _____

Record the time you stop writing: _____

Total number of words you wrote today: _____

Daily writing goal is: _____

Projected ending date: _____

Energy level: _____

Plot your scene above or below the line on a Plot Planner or your own chart.

PROMPT 105

AFFIRMATION PROMPT

The relationship I have with my writing is reflective of my relationship with myself. Daily I honor myself, my writing, and my writing time.

Today I write.

PLOT PROMPT

Conflict between protagonist and antagonist continues to drive the plot. Obstacles fuel the conflict as the main character struggles to reach her goal. As the protagonist nears her goal, the obstacles take on greater and greater levels of difficulty.

During this final sequence, the protagonist may feel as if she has transcended the physical and material world. And transcendence always leads to triumph. The protagonist knows from the experience at the crisis, however, not to be ruled by her ego or become overly confident. She struggles to hold her balance and move forward, step by step, toward the final prize. She is no longer interested in strengthening herself by diminishing others. With increased awareness and new consciousness, and with her ego no longer running her life, she assumes more of her own personal power.

WRITING PROMPT

Look back for an earlier scene in the beginning or the first part of the middle where the protagonist takes some sort of action uniquely her own. Show her remember back to that scene and how she used a certain object or enacted a specific action that worked in the way that it did.

Now, twist the action she used in the beginning in a completely innovative way that reflects all the changes she has undergone. In the glow of success, she recommits to the actions she plans to take to reach the final test.

A wondrous opportunity appears.

RECORD

Record the time you start writing: _____

Record the time you stop writing: _____

Total number of words you wrote today: _____

Daily writing goal is: _____

Projected ending date: _____

Energy level: _____

Plot your scene above or below the line on a Plot Planner or your own chart.

PROMPT 106

AFFIRMATION PROMPT

I do not fight against outside thoughts. I simply notice the distraction and gently continue with my writing. I look forward to this quiet time with my writing.

Today I write.

PLOT PROMPT

The outcomes in the protagonist's life begin to improve internally and externally. She discovers a sense of self-sufficiency. She feels changed from a psychologically immature and emotionally scarred woman to a courageous, self-responsible, and assured individual.

Now the momentum of the story builds swiftly.

This is no time for passivity. Nor is it a time for overly aggressive and controlling action. Instead, the end is a time for innovation and creativity, a time for facing all the external forces of evil. The protagonist sees the world around her through the wisdom she has gained because of the crisis. Now she understands the gift she's been given.

For her, the world is now the same and yet completely different. She realizes that events are not random and arbitrary. Instead they are connected, there to challenge her so she can become strong in anticipation of the climax. Those she viewed through the prism of her old consciousness as antagonists, she now appreciates as teachers.

WRITING PROMPT

No longer isolated, your protagonist more freely expresses her feelings and willingly asks others for help. Show self-mastery with at least one aspect of the self-knowledge and skills she's gained through the appropriate use of her strength of will.

Upon the successful resolution of both an internal and external conflict, reward her with a benefit, one that could be helpful at the climax and is perhaps quite unexpected.

Show her see and understand the larger repercussions of her life upon all other lives. She feels the interconnectedness and unity of all things.

Each time she speaks up, she gathers courage and moves nearer to the final confrontation at the climax.

RECORD

Record the time you start writing: _____

Record the time you stop writing: _____

Total number of words you wrote today: _____

Daily writing goal is: _____

Projected ending date: _____

Energy level: _____

Plot your scene above or below the line on a Plot Planner or your own chart.

PROMPT 107

AFFIRMATION PROMPT

I seize every opportunity I can to write. I am calm and quiet, and under no pressure. My mind is peaceful. I am in a happy mood. I make good gains in my story. I write with confidence.

Today I write.

PLOT PROMPT

The cycles of the Universal Story demand transformation. The more aspects of the protagonist's change you show as it unfolds, the better you demonstrate the depth and breadth of her change. In turn, your story becomes deeper and wider.

WRITING PROMPT

In an earlier scene you wrote for the middle of the story, you showed the protagonist's strength as judged by those she then respected and herself.

Now show her perform the same or similar action. This time, with her new understanding of reality around her, she sees the strength differently than before and demonstrates a use of that strength uniquely her own that reflects who she is now.

 RECORD

Record the time you start writing: _____

Record the time you stop writing: _____

Total number of words you wrote today: _____

Daily writing goal is: _____

Projected ending date: _____

Energy level: _____

Plot your scene above or below the line on a Plot Planner or your own chart.

PROMPT 108

AFFIRMATION PROMPT

My writing restores and strengthens my connection to myself. I neither try to write nor do I not try to write. I simply write in the state of being my true self.

Today I write.

PLOT PROMPT

Toward the end of the book, at the climax, all the major forces come together for a final clash. Your protagonist demonstrates her new awareness, skill, strength, belief, and/or personal power. At the climax, as her new self, she now is able to confront antagonists and conquer challenges that her old self could not.

When she stares down her greatest fear, delivers the gift, and seizes her prize, she wins. And the reader wins.

WRITING PROMPT

Show without a doubt what the protagonist truly fears and why. Show what skills, beliefs, powers, strengths, and/or knowledge she is developing that will serve her well at the point of greatest conflict.

Rather than focus on how she wishes things *were*, the protagonist adjusts to the constant flux around her of how things *are*. She determines what needs to be done and does it.

RECORD

Record the time you start writing: _____

Record the time you stop writing: _____

Total number of words you wrote today: _____

Daily writing goal is: _____

Projected ending date: _____

Energy level: _____

Plot your scene above or below the line on a Plot Planner or your own chart.

PROMPT 109

AFFIRMATION PROMPT

My mind is clear, like a glass mirror reflecting words back honestly—not too much, not too little, and with no interference.

Today I write.

PLOT PROMPT

The thematic significance reflects the story's own view about life and how people behave. After a draft or two or three, you begin to understand the themes of your story and what they add up to in the end.

The process of coaxing one thematic significance statement out of an entire project requires patience.

WRITING PROMPT

Explore and develop in several scenes the broader meaning and message your story conveys about life or society, and ultimately about human nature.

Bring a sense of fullness and closure to any plot threads you developed in earlier scenes and lost track of. Consider leaving the resolution of one of the subplots hanging. Bring meaning here and now.

Show the protagonist begin to doubt herself. She keeps on going even while wondering if what she's doing is the right thing to do.

✍ RECORD

Record the time you start writing: _____

Record the time you stop writing: _____

Total number of words you wrote today: _____

Daily writing goal is: _____

Projected ending date: _____

Energy level: _____

Plot your scene above or below the line on a Plot Planner or your own chart.

PROMPT 110

AFFIRMATION PROMPT

I write the words I feel. I am not in a hurry. I have no schedule to follow, no agenda to fill. I owe nothing and ask for nothing. I am fulfilled and at peace when I write.

Today I write.

PLOT PROMPT

The dramatic meaning of your piece comes from scenes that are played out moment-by-moment on the page through action and dialogue. The emotional meaning always comes from the characters. The thematic meaning ties your entire story together. It's the reason you write your story, what you hope to prove, what the story is about. Theme is beneath the apparent subject or surface of the story; it is the deeper subject you are exploring.

Of course, there is always a lot more going on in a story than just the one- or two-sentence description of the theme, but a thematic significance statement attempts to represent the primary essence of your story.

WRITING PROMPT

The moment the protagonist takes the first step toward the completion of her final goal, she struggles to take full ownership of her newly discovered consciousness.

Create a scene around action that shows her rescue someone or something struggling, or doing something for the pure joy of doing it. Some of her actions are from leftover bad habits, and she becomes more and more painfully aware each time her actions or speech do not align with her new understanding of herself and the world around her.

Alert about her surroundings, she notices what's going on. She watches what others say and do. She spots mistakes as they occur. Then she refocuses on what needs to be done right now, shares control, and does it.

RECORD

Record the time you start writing: _____

Record the time you stop writing: _____

Total number of words you wrote today: _____

Daily writing goal is: _____

Projected ending date: _____

Energy level: _____

Plot your scene above or below the line on a Plot Planner or your own chart.

PROMPT 111

AFFIRMATION PROMPT

In these last-quarter scenes, as my protagonist begins to develop and rely on her intuition, I do as well. I bring more discipline to my writing schedule. I trust the process of discovery and myself. I keep my eye on my goal, knowing how near I am to success.

Today I write.

PLOT PROMPT

Even after the rest and reflection time spent at the threshold, the full integration of what is happening to your character involves an adjustment period. She is cracked open. A blinding light floods into every part of her. She needs practice incorporating the depth and breadth of learning and connectedness into her being. She has not yet mastered her transformation. She may require one step forward, two steps back, and three forward on her way to the climax.

WRITING PROMPT

Show the protagonist taking steps toward her goal. As she does, she makes mistakes. The parts of her old self most threatened by her new will continue to dog her. Each time she finds herself sinking into old patterns, she grasps onto a bit of wisdom she has learned throughout the story.

Her new insights about herself are like life rafts to remind her of who she is becoming. They bring her strength. In preparation for the climax, she rids herself of all extraneous possessions and people.

✎ RECORD

Record the time you start writing: _____

Record the time you stop writing: _____

Total number of words you wrote today: _____

Daily writing goal is: _____

Projected ending date: _____

Energy level: _____

Plot your scene above or below the line on a Plot Planner or your own chart.

PROMPT 112

AFFIRMATION PROMPT

With a clear mind, I do not think in language; I feel. I feel my story. I feel the characters. I feel the words. Today, I clear my mind and let the writing flow.

Today I write.

PLOT PROMPT

Consciousness does not mean that your protagonist will always be strong and confident, that she will show up consistently to do what needs to be done and believe in herself. Mastery means that she knows herself well enough now to use new strategies to pick herself out of the muck more quickly and with fewer bruises.

WRITING PROMPT

Show the protagonist rediscover and reclaim parts of her true self as she becomes conscious of the illusion she has been living under her entire life because of her backstory wound.

Show her release old beliefs that were developed as a defense mechanism and discover an important piece of what she truly believes and who she truly is. Show her receive news or experience evidence of the growing forces gathering against her.

 RECORD

Record the time you start writing: _____

Record the time you stop writing: _____

Total number of words you wrote today: _____

Daily writing goal is: _____

Projected ending date: _____

Energy level: _____

Plot your scene above or below the line on a Plot Planner or your own chart.

PROMPT 113

AFFIRMATION PROMPT

When I sit down to write, I let go of the material world that surrounds me. I take my time. When I write, I am fulfilled and at peace, fully aware and alive.

Today I write.

PLOT PROMPT

Internal, character-driven stories end more reflectively than external, dramatic-action stories. Now, the protagonist stops making decisions based on what she "should do" according to an old belief system, society, or family and recreating situations that keep her stuck. She is no longer obedient and dependent, expecting and receiving punishments and rewards. She refuses to adhere to what she ought to do, how she should behave, and the expectations of other people. Instead, she follows her intuition, listens to herself, and opens herself to guidance.

The protagonist is determined now to make a stand in her life and live her truth. Because of this, the antagonists in her life intensify their resistance to her change and growth. Their refusal turns up the heat. The character has to stretch. Because she stretches, she makes mistakes and sometimes fails again. The emotion of the story rises higher.

The more mistakes the protagonist makes listening to her own heart and expressing her true emotions, the more she learns. Only now, she does not attach energy or emotion to her problems. Rather than reacting and creating more difficulty, she detaches. No longer dragging around a sack full of old issues, she is free and often finds herself almost floating.

Her earlier goal or outer purpose expands into something much larger now that she is empowered by consciousness. No longer desperate, her feelings of isolation, competition, and separation vanish. With a new sense of insight and appreciation of the greater mystery, she understands every act has consequences in the world at large. Her decision-making process becomes more certain and takes less time. She relies less on gathering and analyzing data and more on intuition and instinct.

WRITING PROMPT

Show, in a scene, the protagonist begin to assume her full power and how this shift in her threatens family members, coworkers, and/or friends. Show how her piece of the puzzle changes and how that causes a readjustment of the entire picture, the total scheme.

Show those around her unsettled, perplexed, irritable, anxious, and afraid of change because they refuse to accept her change. Show how their refusal intensifies the emotional tension. Show how the protagonist has to stretch. Show her make mistakes and even fall back into old patterns, only now she is aware of what she is doing to herself.

Show her earlier goal or outer purpose expand into something much larger now that she is empowered by consciousness. She's going to do whatever it is she's planning on doing anyway; she thinks to herself, why not really go for it?

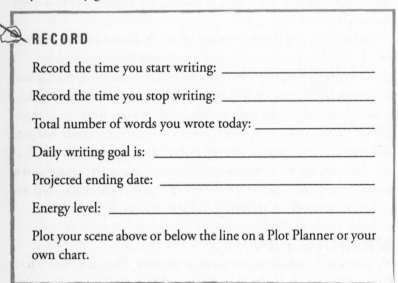

RECORD

Record the time you start writing: _____

Record the time you stop writing: _____

Total number of words you wrote today: _____

Daily writing goal is: _____

Projected ending date: _____

Energy level: _____

Plot your scene above or below the line on a Plot Planner or your own chart.

PROMPT 114

AFFIRMATION PROMPT

In the moments I write in scene, I live in the power of now.

Today I write.

PLOT PROMPT

Before the true climax, often the antagonist who the protagonist believes is her greatest foe challenges her again. Unlike earlier encounters, this time the protagonist is assertive instead of aggressive. Now she incorporates everything she has learned. She turns the opposing energy into something helpful. Because of all the antagonists she has confronted in the story and learned from along the way, at the climax the character believes she is able to show us yet another way to live life in triumph.

For many protagonists, especially those in character-driven stories, the character's backstory represents the loss of the imperfect imprint of her original self. In other words, something happens to the protagonist that causes her to begin to doubt herself and to fear the world around her.

Because of all the dramatic action that takes place in the front story, by the climax the protagonist has uncovered and rediscovered her perfect imprint. In realigning herself to her inner purpose, for the first time since the backstory robbed her of herself, she meets herself as she is truly meant to be. She may fear what she faces at the climax, but she no longer runs away from her fears. She confronts them head-on.

WRITING PROMPT

The entire story is building to one epic moment. The reader will expect the protagonist to take center stage at the climax of the story, facing her greatest foe, fear, antagonist, villain, and/or enemy.

Show both the protagonist and the person or thing she believes holds a piece of the power she wishes now to reclaim. Show them as they move toward a confrontation.

If what happens at the climax is violent, foreshadow violence now (as hopefully you have done earlier in the story, too). Remind the reader of an important detail. Make clear now anything needed by the reader to fully appreciate the climax to come.

RECORD

Record the time you start writing: _____

Record the time you stop writing: _____

Total number of words you wrote today: _____

Daily writing goal is: _____

Projected ending date: _____

Energy level: _____

Plot your scene above or below the line on a Plot Planner or your own chart.

PROMPT 115

AFFIRMATION PROMPT

I write daily with my honest self as best and simply as I can. Every day I write, my words more clearly communicate the story as it wants to be told. Each time I write, I go further into my story and reconnect with a deep part of myself.

Today I write.

PLOT PROMPT

Each scene delivers more tension and conflict than the preceding scene and builds to the story's climax. Think of your story as energy that rises to each of the energetic markers and falls after each of those turning points, only to rise again even higher at the next major scene. You have chosen where and when to direct the flow of your scenes and how to encourage the energy to crest and fall for the greatest emotional impact.

Now, at the end, you approach the energetic surge that holds power enough to turn the dramatic action of the story in an entirely new direction, create a whole new level of intensity in the story, and contribute to its thematic significance.

WRITING PROMPT

Before the climax, the point of highest drama in your story, is the crowning moment when the thematic significance of your story becomes clear to the reader. At first it looks as if all is permanently lost for the protagonist. Show your protagonist confront what she believes is her true antagonist and fail.

RECORD

Record the time you start writing: _____

Record the time you stop writing: _____

Total number of words you wrote today: _____

Daily writing goal is: _____

Projected ending date: _____

Energy level: _____

Plot your scene above or below the line on a Plot Planner or your own chart.

PROMPT 116

AFFIRMATION PROMPT

Every day I write, I clear the way for my muse to offer words that best communicate my story.

Today I write.

PLOT PROMPT

The fourth energetic marker holds the greatest intensity and highest drama in the entire story. Prepare yourself for the climax. You have one prompt to get your protagonist to center stage at the climax of the story, ready to face her greatest foe, fear, antagonist, villain, and/or enemy.

She is transformed—herself but a different self—thanks to every one of the dramatic-action scenes she survived earlier in the story.

WRITING PROMPT

Ask yourself: Which scene most dramatically shows your protagonist demonstrating her transformed self? Which antagonist most represents what she needs to reclaim in herself? Which antagonist gives the most thematic significance to the climax? Get it/him/her there.

Where is the exactly right place for the protagonist to face this most powerful antagonist? Get her there.

RECORD

Record the time you start writing: _____

Record the time you stop writing: _____

Total number of words you wrote today: _____

Daily writing goal is: _____

Projected ending date: _____

Energy level: _____

Plot your scene above or below the line on a Plot Planner or your own chart.

PROMPT 117

AFFIRMATION PROMPT

By writing every day, I have increased my strength and expanded my vision. I daily support longer-lasting energy and light for my writing and my story. Today, I am strong and I see far.

Today I write.

PLOT PROMPT

The action taken at the climax by the protagonist answers the dramatic question posed at the beginning of the story: Will she or won't she be victorious? At the climax, all major conflicts are resolved. The energy of the entire story crescendos at the climax and immediately is defused.

The climax does not have to be full of explosions and death. What this most important scene must have is *meaning to the overall story*.

The actions required of the protagonist at the climax would have been too much for her anywhere else in the story. She first needed to go through the experiences described in the story in order to prevail at the climax. Now, the moment is all hers.

Beginnings hook readers. Endings create fans.

WRITING PROMPT

Your protagonist faces her greatest foe, fear, antagonist, villain, and/or enemy. Show her doing something she could not have done anywhere else in the story.

Just when it looks as if all is permanently lost for the protagonist, she displays rediscovered or refined awareness, skill, and/or knowledge. Make her action demonstrate the special skill, ability, insight, or knowledge she gained from all the conflict along the way in the story. In other words, show how she needed to go through every scene in order to be transformed into who she is now and act in a pivotal way to face her foe and banish her fear.

Choose what to include and what not to include in your climax by focusing on the details: how that moment feels, tastes, and smells. How does the protagonist look at her moment of triumph, and what does she do? Specific is always better than general.

Let the thematic significance or deeper meaning of the story dictate the final layer in the selection, organization, nuances, and details of the climax.

✎ RECORD

Record the time you start writing: _____

Record the time you stop writing: _____

Total number of words you wrote today: _____

Daily writing goal is: _____

Projected ending date: _____

Energy level: _____

Plot your scene above or below the line on a Plot Planner or your own chart.

PROMPT 118

AFFIRMATION PROMPT

My writing has given me wisdom to search for the truth, my truth, the story I dream of sharing with readers. As my story has grown in strength, I have, too. Together, we have expanded our range of sight and meaning.

Today I write.

PLOT PROMPT

The protagonist is always the one to initiate the final clash at the climax. Something meaningful happens both within the protagonist and to the outer situation, as well as in the interaction between the protagonist and her greatest fear. Quickly thereafter, however, she may find she needs help.

WRITING PROMPT

Show a secondary character step in to help the protagonist finish off what she started at the climax.

✍ RECORD

Record the time you start writing: _____

Record the time you stop writing: _____

Total number of words you wrote today: _____

Daily writing goal is: _____

Projected ending date: _____

Energy level: _____

Plot your scene above or below the line on a Plot Planner or your own chart.

PROMPT 119

AFFIRMATION PROMPT

My story reflects meaning from all directions. It cuts through, sees through, and connects to everything. My writing drives my life force.

Today I write.

PLOT PROMPT

The story reached its pinnacle, the culmination of all the energy that came before the climax. The protagonist's actions relieved the pressure that had been building within the story and provided a cathartic release. Consequently, now the energy of the story immediately drops, as reflected on the final downward line of the Plot Planner for the resolution.

A story cannot continue for many pages after the goal is met at the climax. As soon as the story question is answered, the tension vanishes.

The resolution of a story is the sum of the character's actions. It gives the reader a sense of what the story world looks like now that the protagonist has been transformed.

Whatever name you give it, the final chapter shows the protagonist making peace with the past and returning to a right relationship with herself and the world around her.

Usually an ally realizes her goal as well. That goal may feed into the protagonist's goal, supporting and emphasizing it.

WRITING PROMPT

Show an ally achieve her goal.

RECORD

Record the time you start writing: _____

Record the time you stop writing: _____

Total number of words you wrote today: _____

Daily writing goal is: _____

Projected ending date: _____

Energy level: _____

Plot your scene above or below the line on a Plot Planner or your own chart.

PROMPT 120

AFFIRMATION PROMPT

Everything is working out for my highest good and for the highest good of my story. All my daily writing has given me my dream. Today, I hold my book in my hands.

Today I write.

PLOT PROMPT

The energy of the story drops after the climax because the primary story question of *transformation* has been answered. However, deliberately leaving an unanswered question or two beyond the primary plot helps guarantee that the energy of the story will live on in the reader even after the last page.

Leaving loose ends of subplots invites reader involvement and interaction. A bond develops between the reader and the story, which often leads to loyal fans.

The details surrounding her at the resolution reveal the protagonist's truth. Details—hers and hers alone—deepen the reader's understanding of who the character is now and reflect her ultimate transformation.

WRITING PROMPT

At the beginning of your story, you introduced a dream your protagonist had for her future. At first in the middle, you added another layer to that dream. Later in the middle, you added a glimpse of someone helpful or a bit of magic that could possibly make that dream a reality.

The realization of her dream now comes as a surprise; though because of the subtle foreshadowing you did earlier, it also feels inevitable to the reader and thematically true to the story. The realization of her dream coming true now acts as a twist in resolving the story.

Show the protagonist and the details of the world around her as they naturally appear now.

✎ RECORD

Record the time you start writing: _____

Record the time you stop writing: _____

Total number of words you wrote today: _____

Daily writing goal is: _____

Projected ending date: _____

Energy level: _____

Plot the scene above the line on your Plot Planner and label it as the "End of the Climax and Resolution" scene.

CONCLUSION

I have always been fascinated by energy, which is why the Universal Story so delights me. I love the idea of an energetic path that cycles through the beginning and the end of a story, and everything else in life, too. Sometimes the energy builds and sometimes it fades, like the waves near my house. You can't force a story to come any more than you can force a wave to break.

At the same time I'm writing this book of prompts, I am also promoting the official release of *The Plot Whisperer Workbook: Step-by-Step Exercises to Help You Write Compelling Stories*. I chuckle as I write this, grateful now for the ebb in my energy when it came time to plan the promotion. If I had been at the same energetic spot I was ten months earlier for the release of *The Plot Whisperer: Secrets of Story Structure Any Writer Can Master*, I would be in big trouble right now. By following the energy at the time and not pushing, I've now got more energy, more free time to write, and so much less stress to the point that I'm beginning to believe I may actually achieve the deadline I've been given for *The Plot Whisperer Book of Writing Prompts*.

When I tell friends and family about my deadline, everyone gasps—three weeks to deliver a book. Invariably, they then immediately switch to calling out examples of writing prompts used in the usual way.

Write a description of what you're seeing outside your window. Be specific and detailed, including shapes, colors, action, smells, sounds, and so on. Put it aside for an hour and then go back and read it again. How much has changed outside your window? How can you capture that change in your writing?

Write the first fifty words that come into your head. Don't think about them; just write them down as fast as you can. Now write a paragraph or several paragraphs using as many of them as you can.

Imagine having lunch with your protagonist at the stage they've reached in your story. Write a short description of the lunch: What would you eat, what would you wear, where would you have your meal, and what would you talk about?

These are fine prompts that inspire a free flow of ideas and stimulate the imagination to write. However, as I see it, this approach leaves a writer with stacks of journals or piles of scrap paper filled with short snippets, lovely descriptions, and clever word pairings that all add up to . . . a whole bunch of words. My plan has been to provide specific suggestions that inspire and stimulate your imagination to write just as many words; only with my method, you'll be left with a meaningful story from beginning to end—a book.

Some writers I work with have such vivid imaginations that it's difficult to rein in all their ideas and teach them how to stay focused on one particular story at a time. Others have focus and passion but struggle when it comes to knowing what to write about and how to generate one scene after another.

When writers hear about this book and they throw off suggestions, I hear what sounds a bit like trepidation crouching behind their fixation on the traditional use of writing prompts as a means to stimulate creativity. What some writers seem to be saying is that they think they don't have an imagination—or if they do, their creativity is not good enough. They speak as if they are afraid of not having in them the ability to create something from nothing.

I offer my ideas to the girl who asks her mother what she should dream about at night. What the little girl doesn't appreciate about herself yet is that she doesn't need her mother to tell her what to dream about any more than you need me to tell you what to write about. You already know. I'm merely whispering encouragement along the way and providing plot parameters to remind you of what goes where in a book with a plot.

Today I write.

—*September 2012*

INDEX